My love flowers

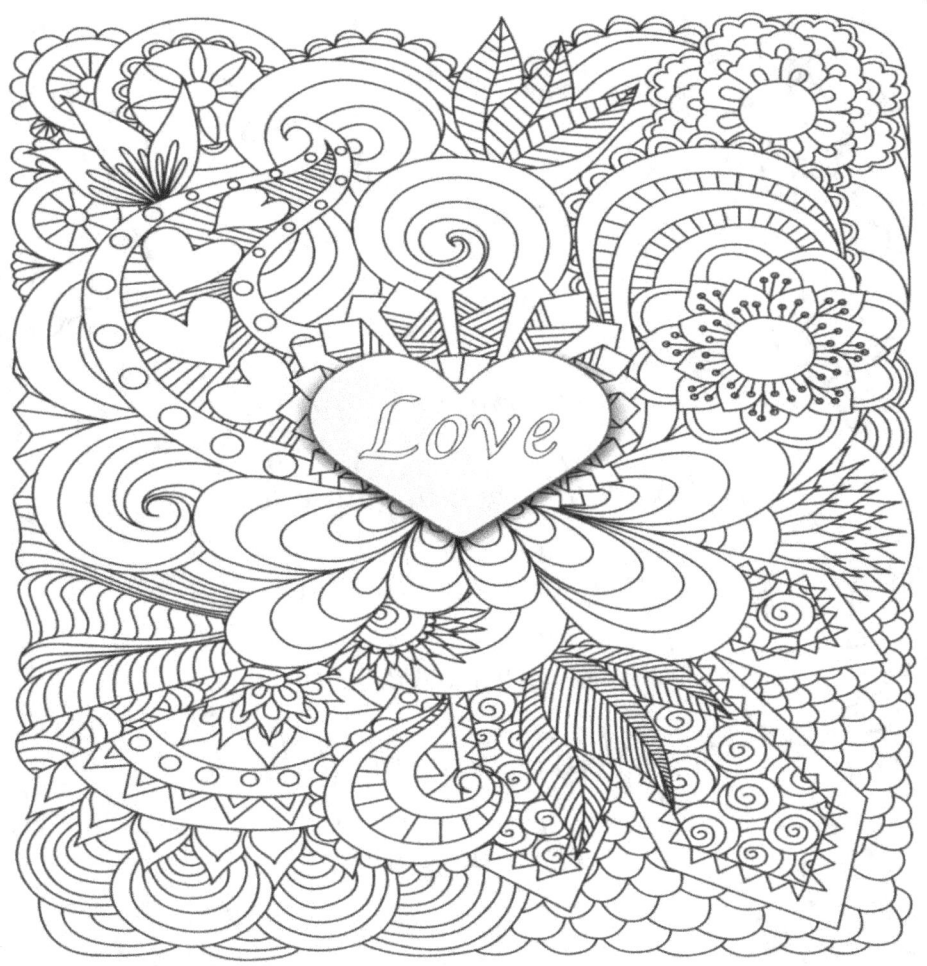

This book belongs to

_____

_____

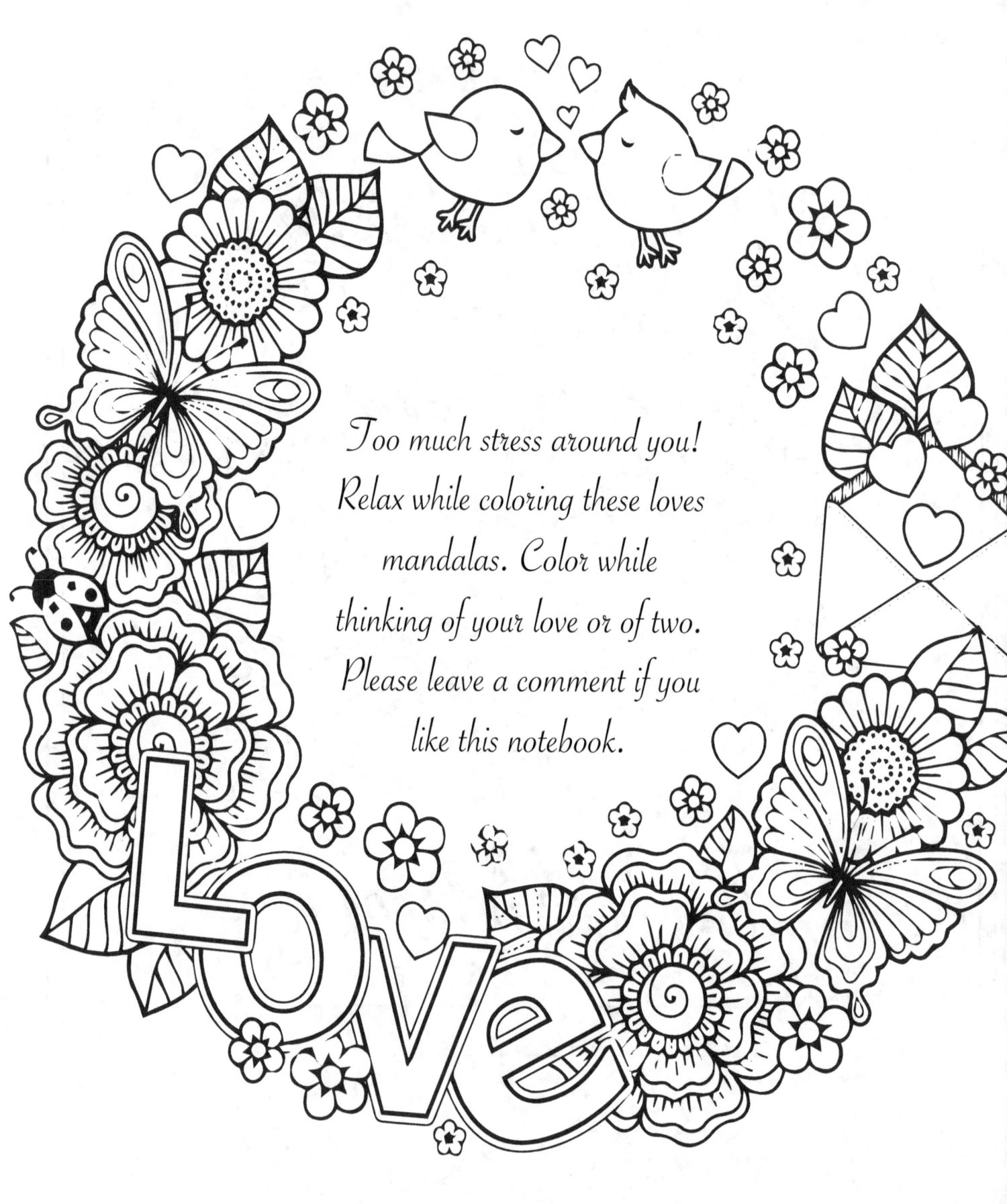

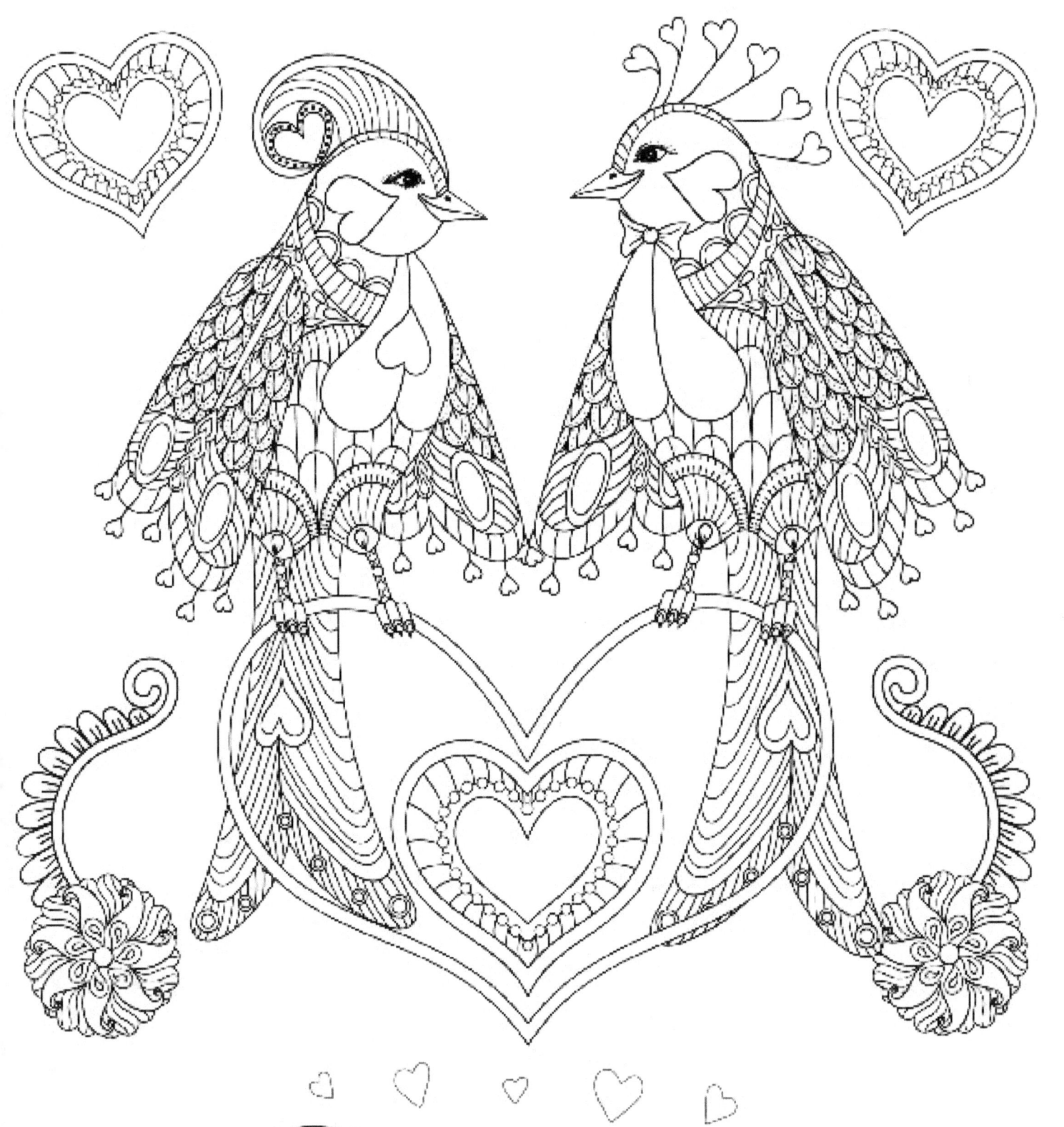

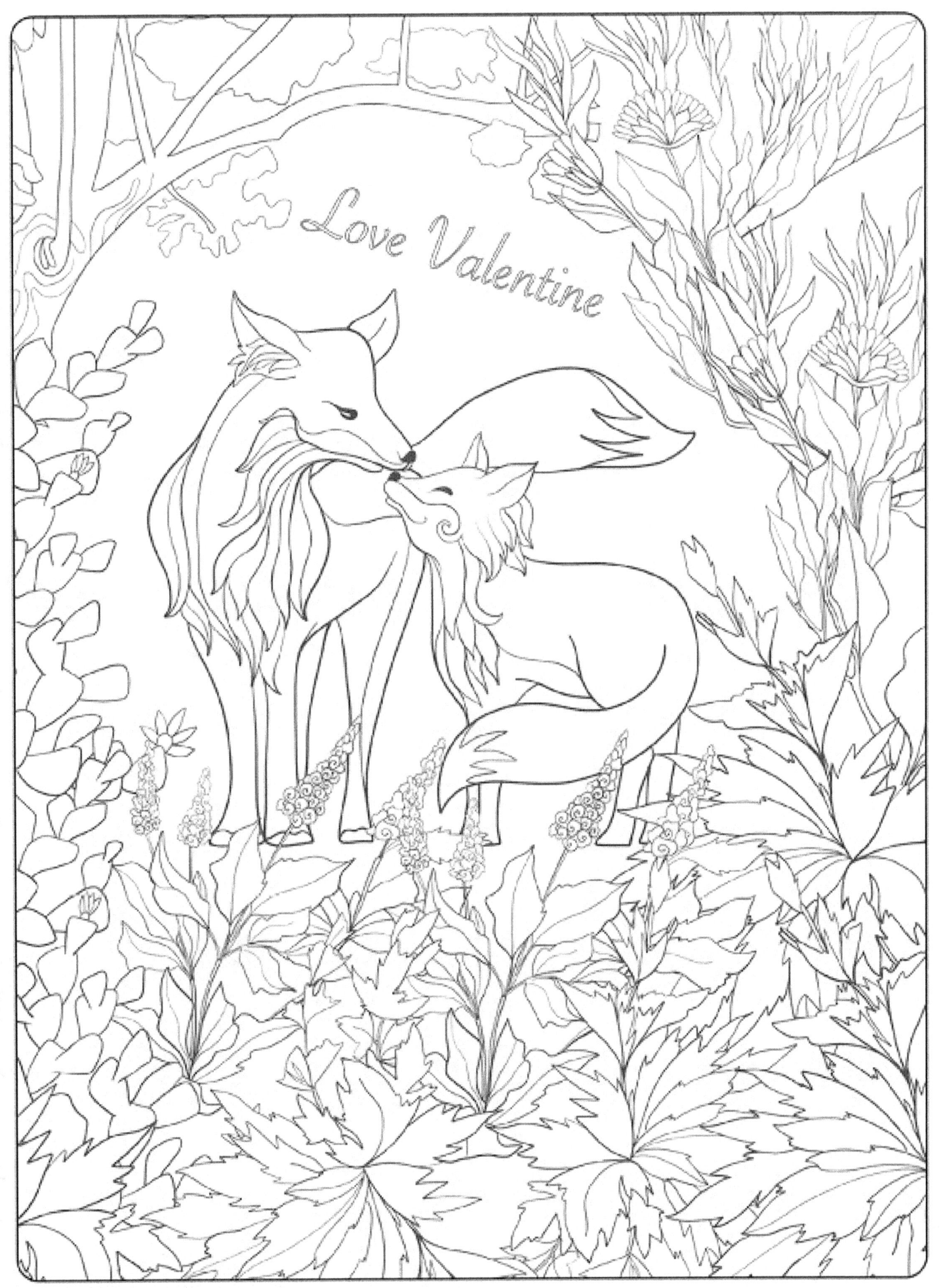

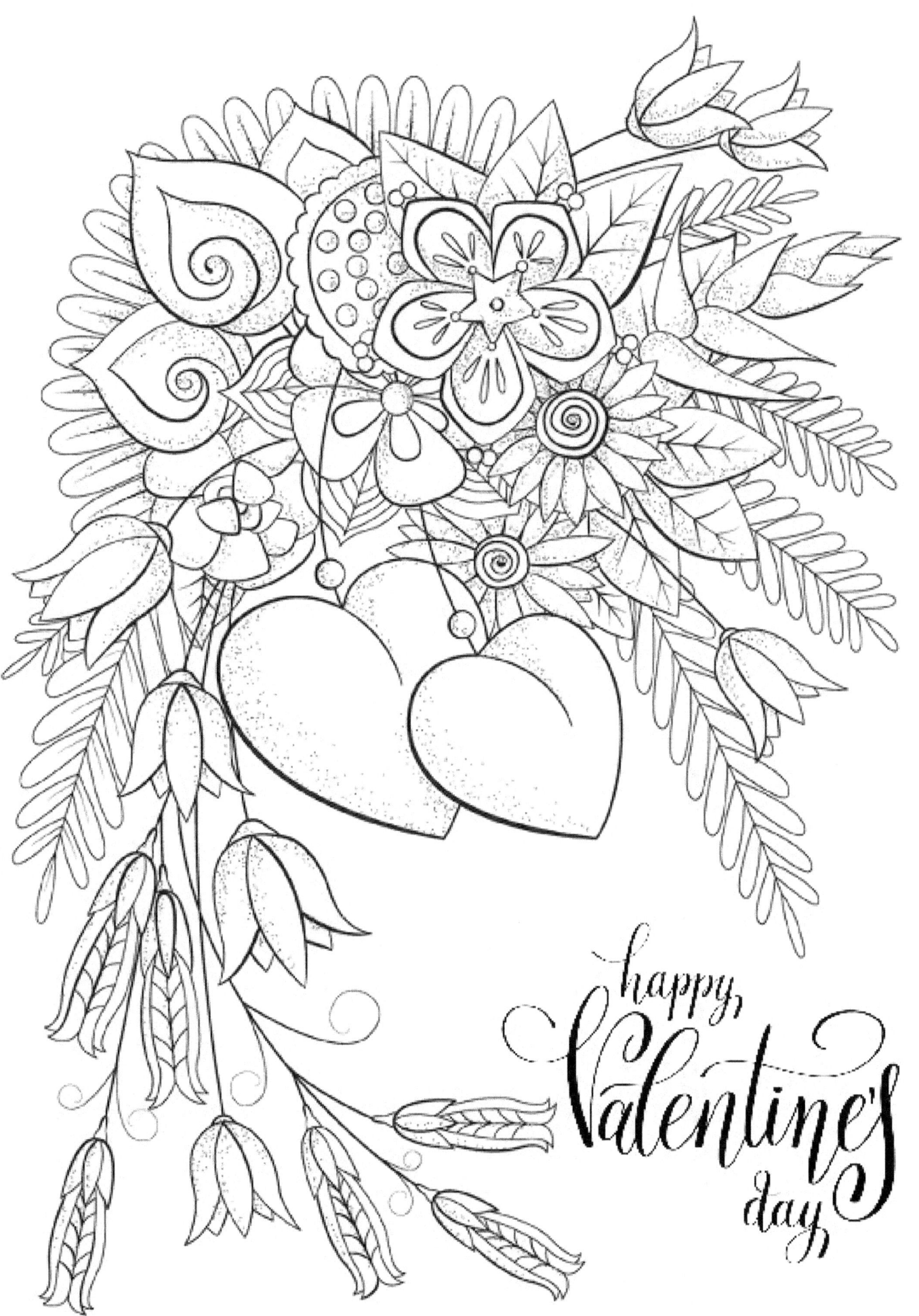

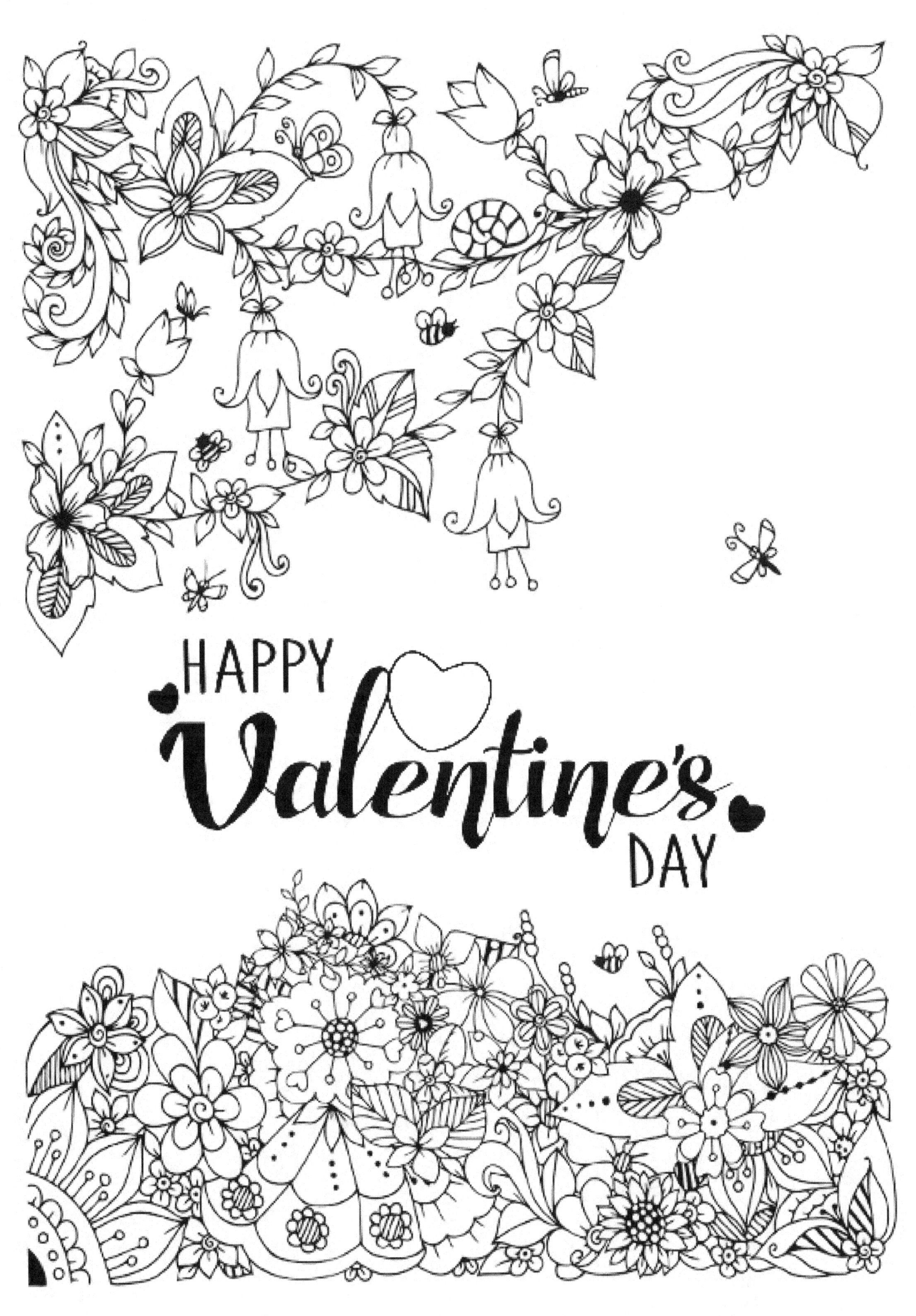

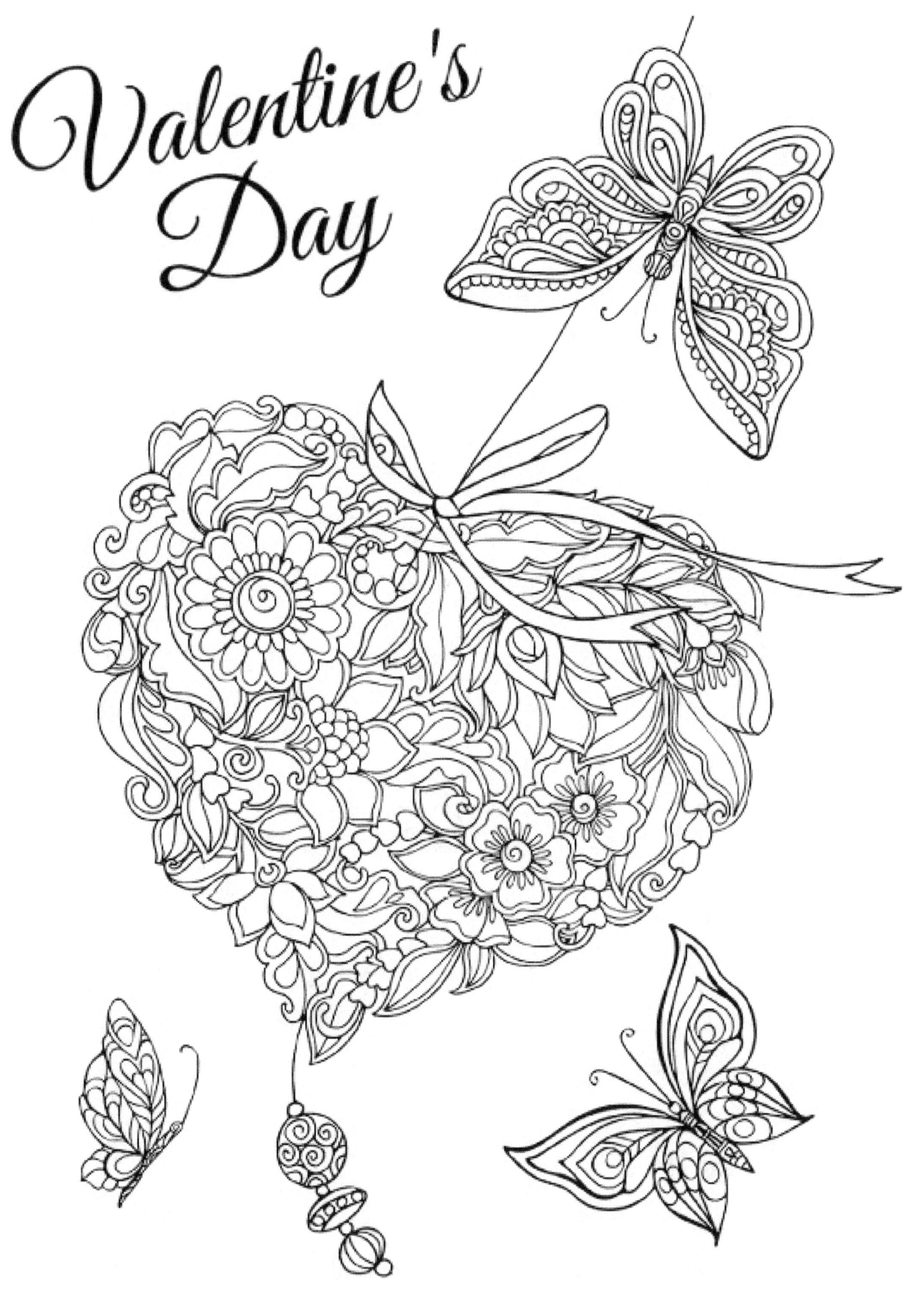

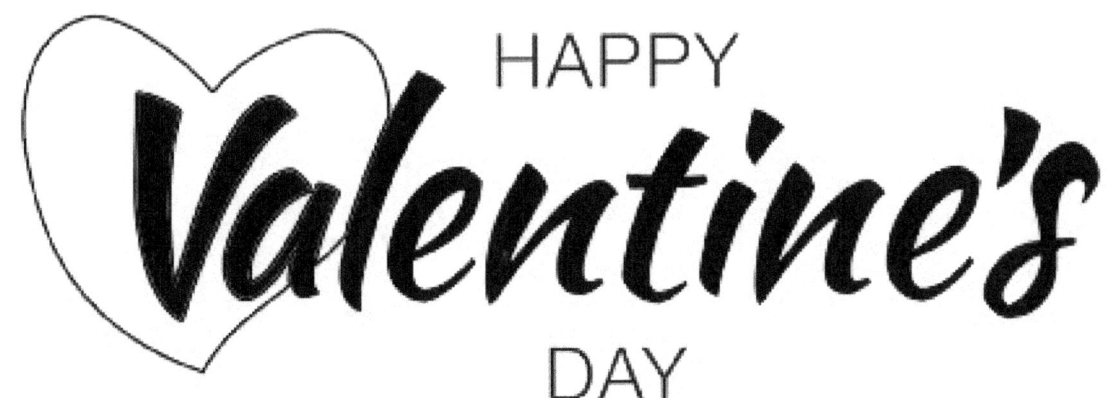

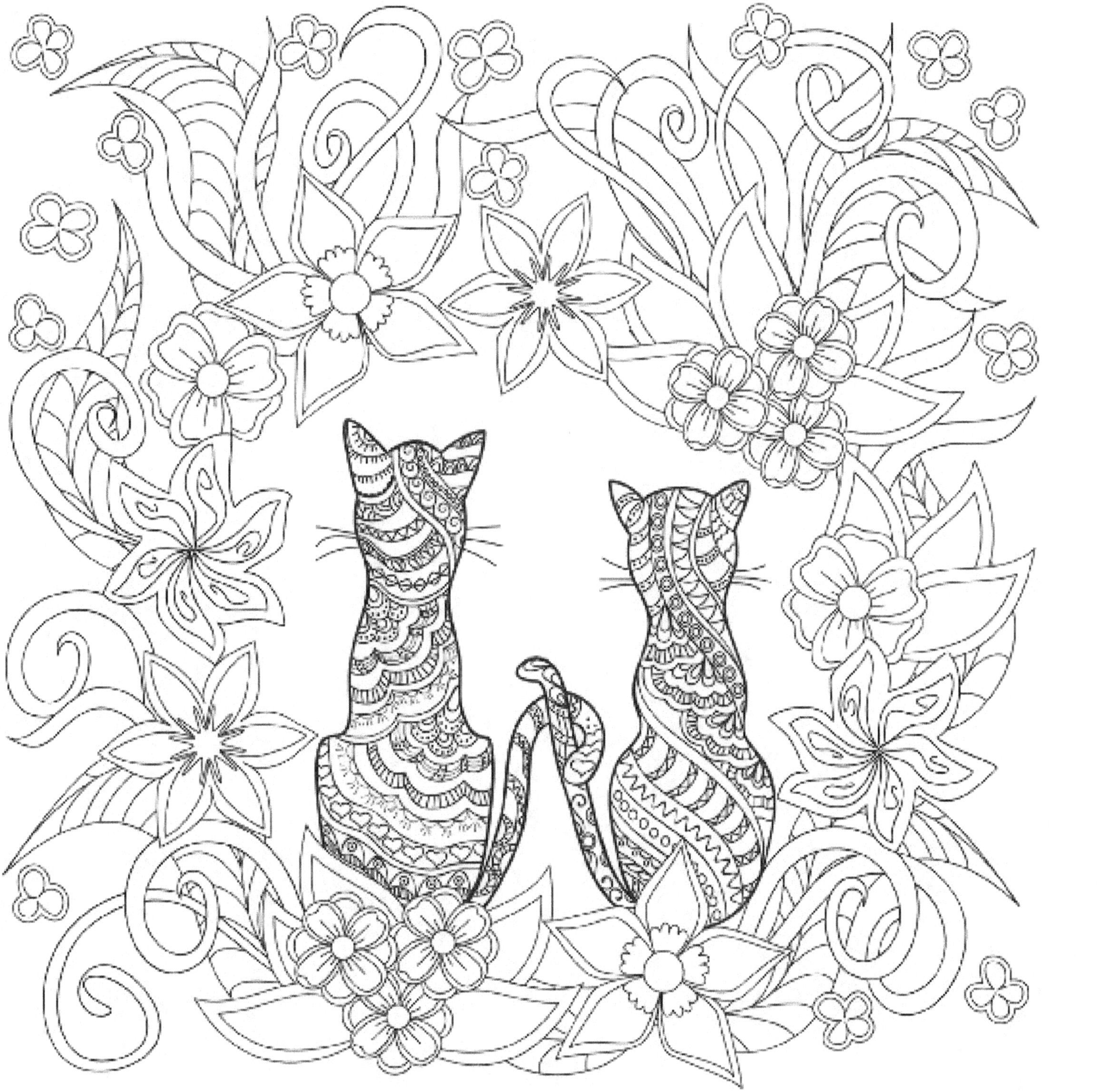

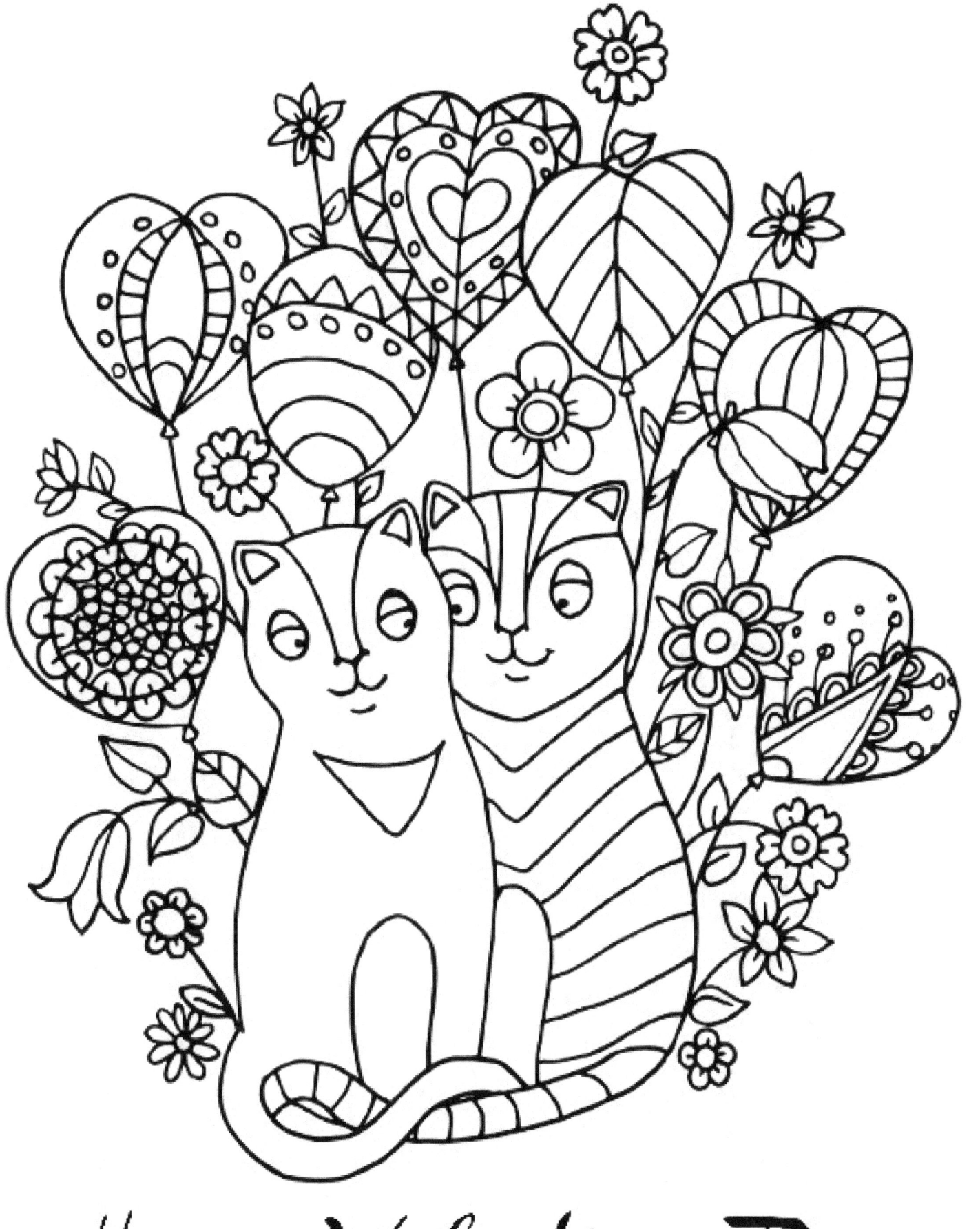

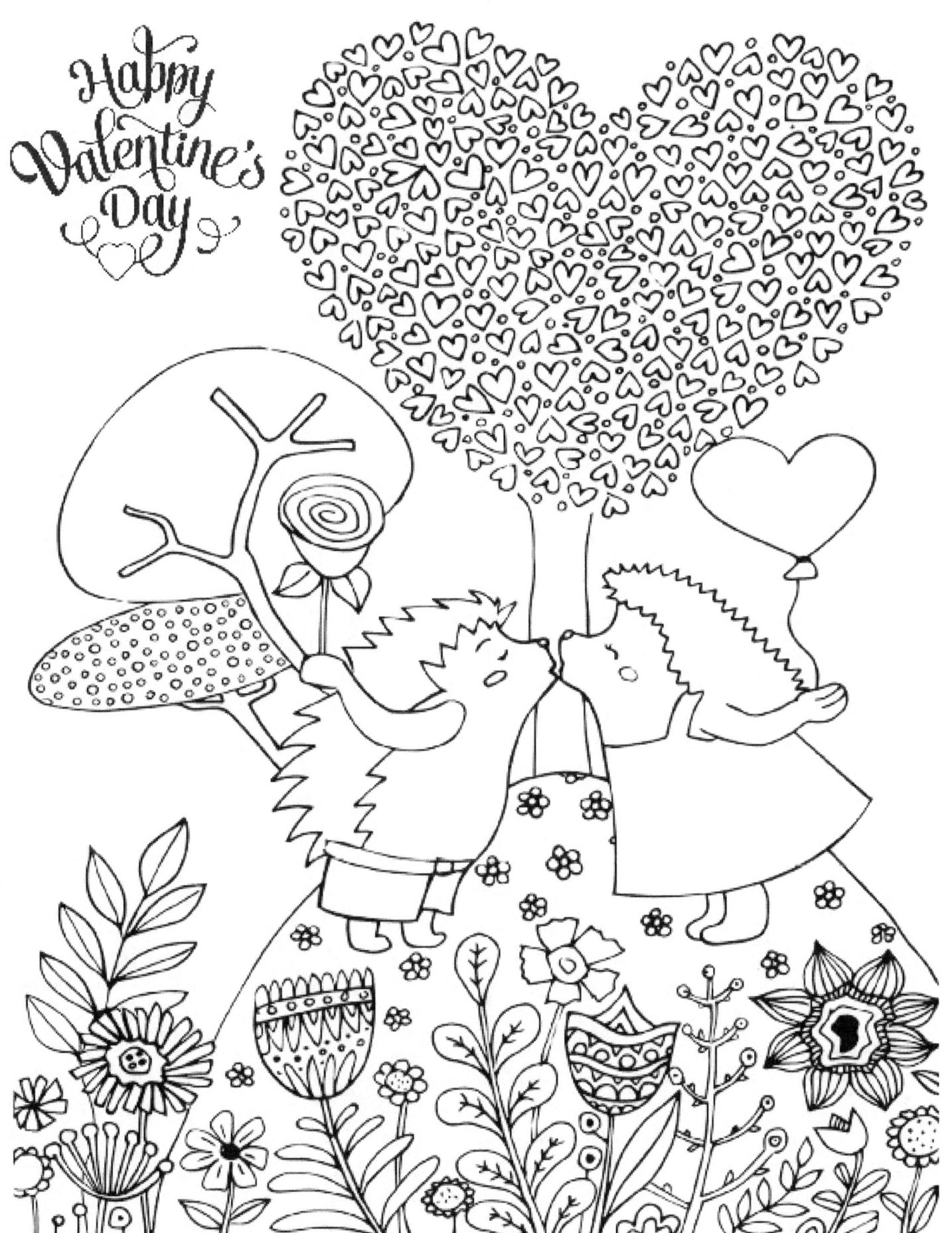

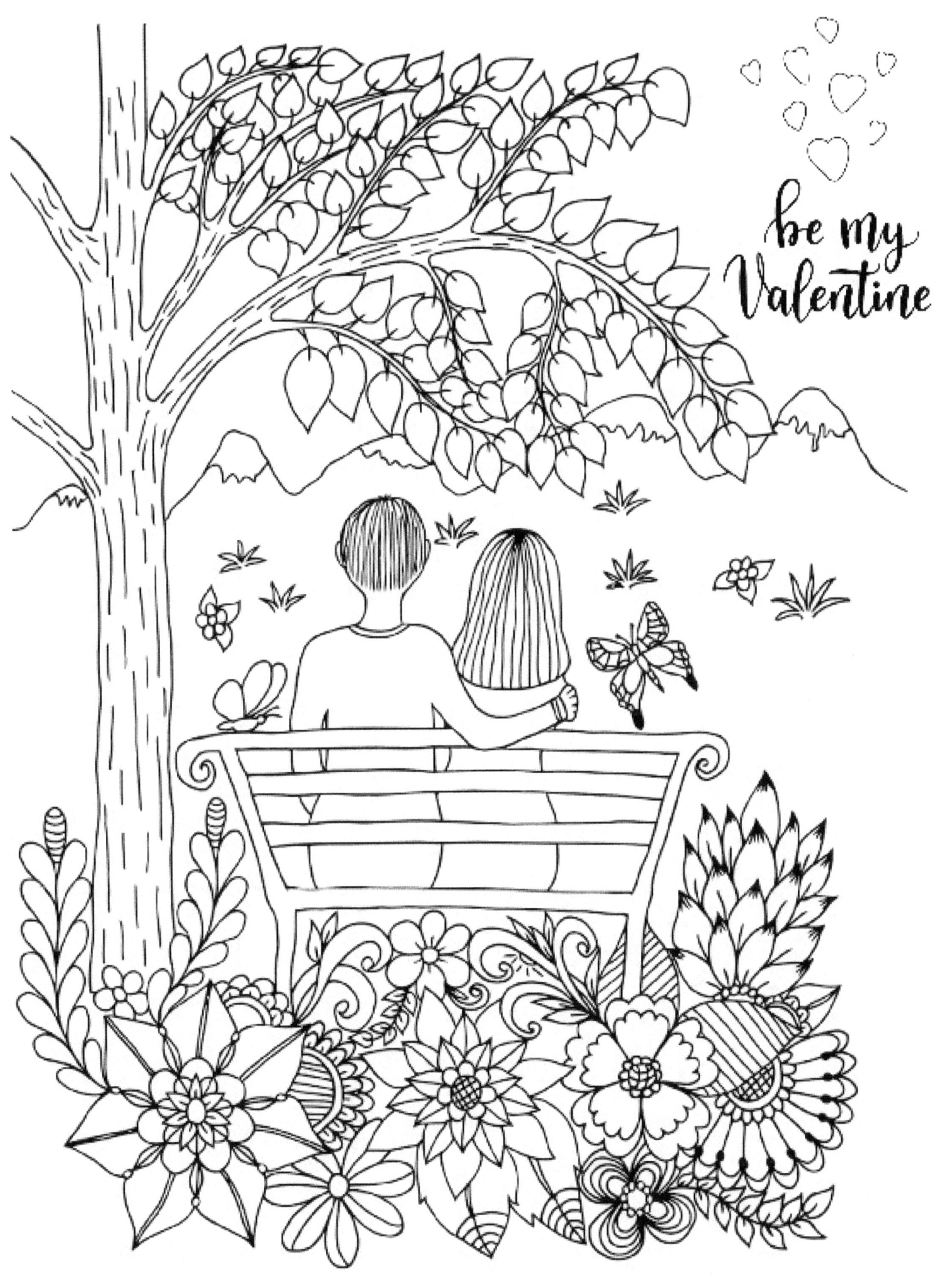

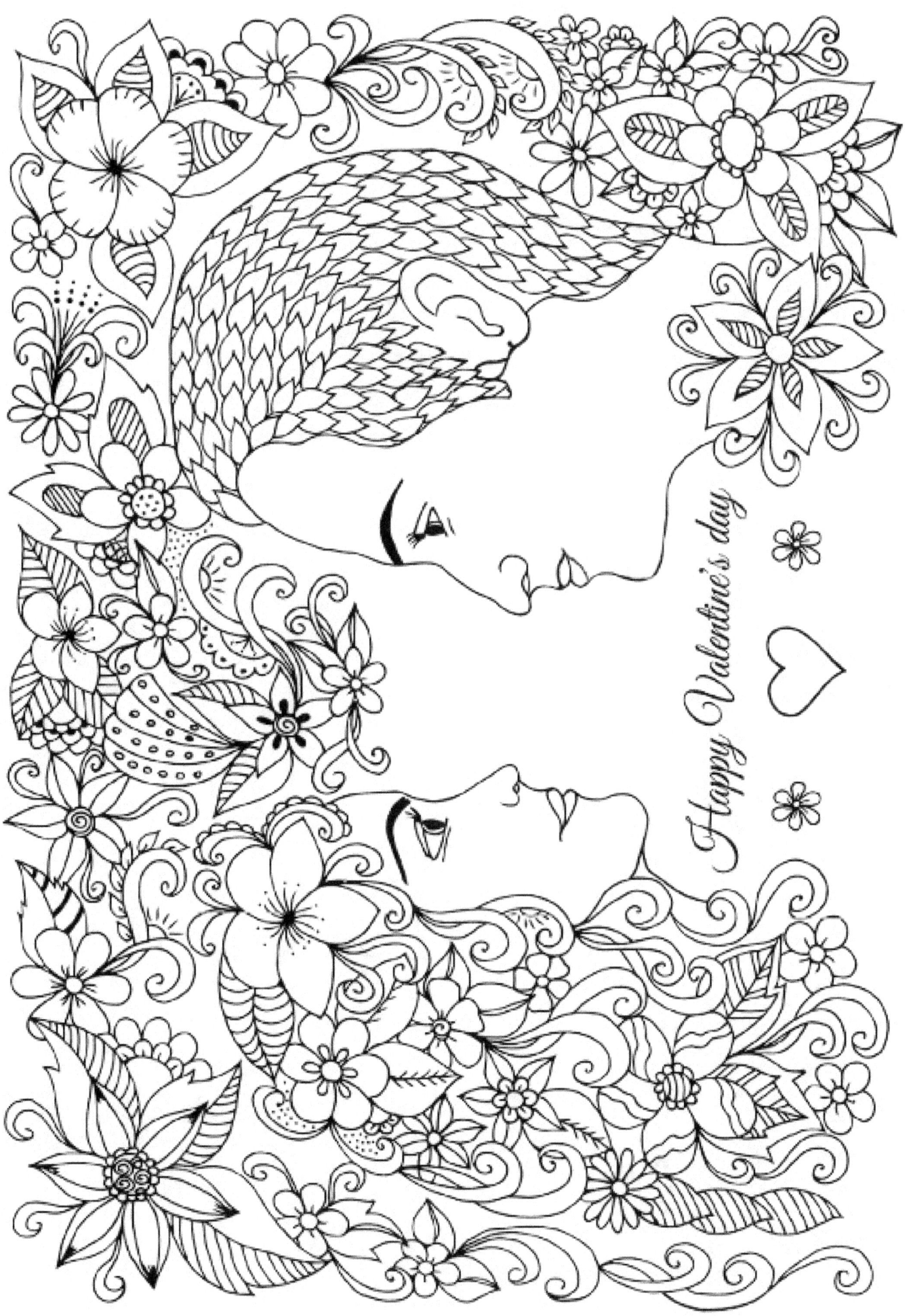

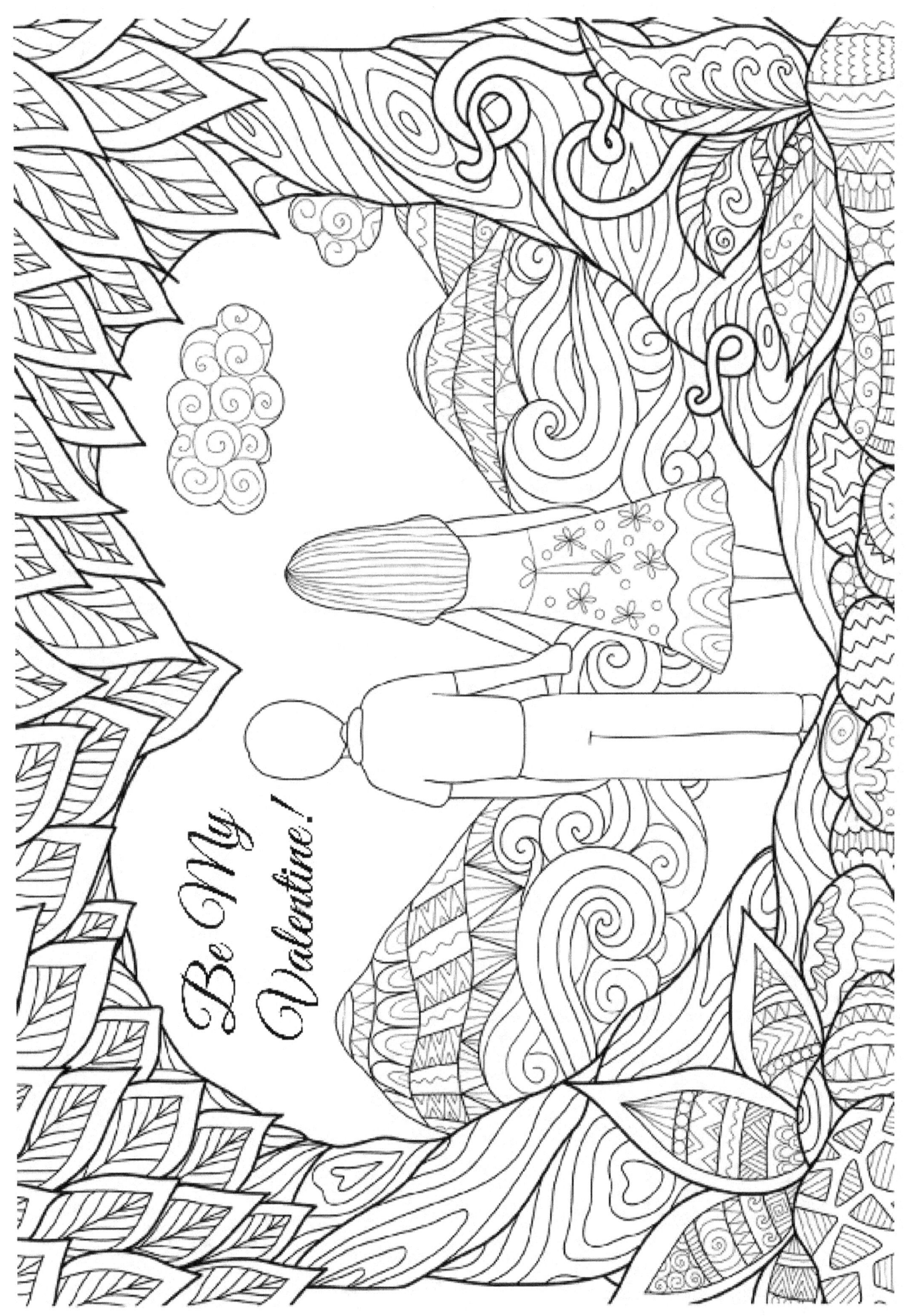

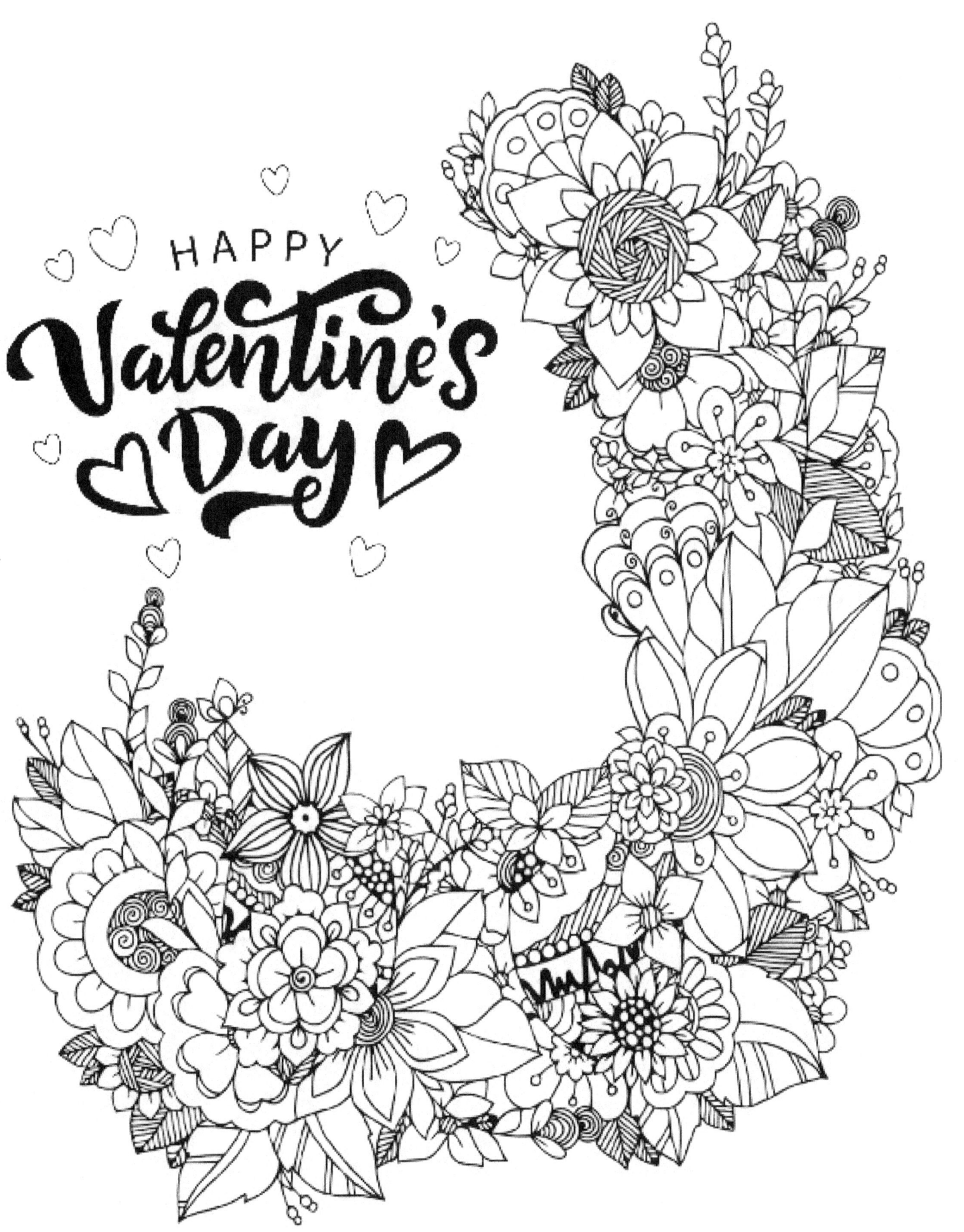

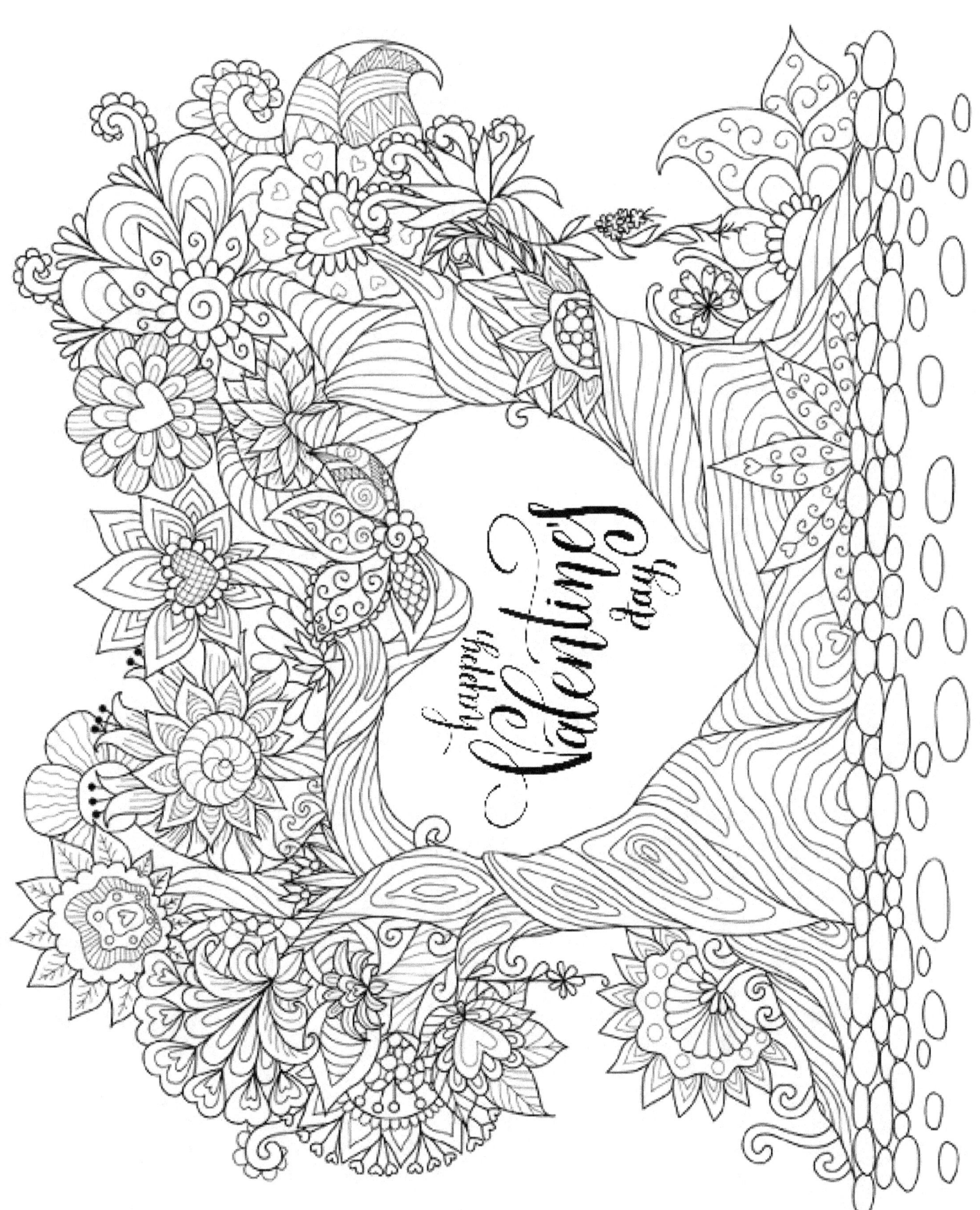

Happy Valentines Day!

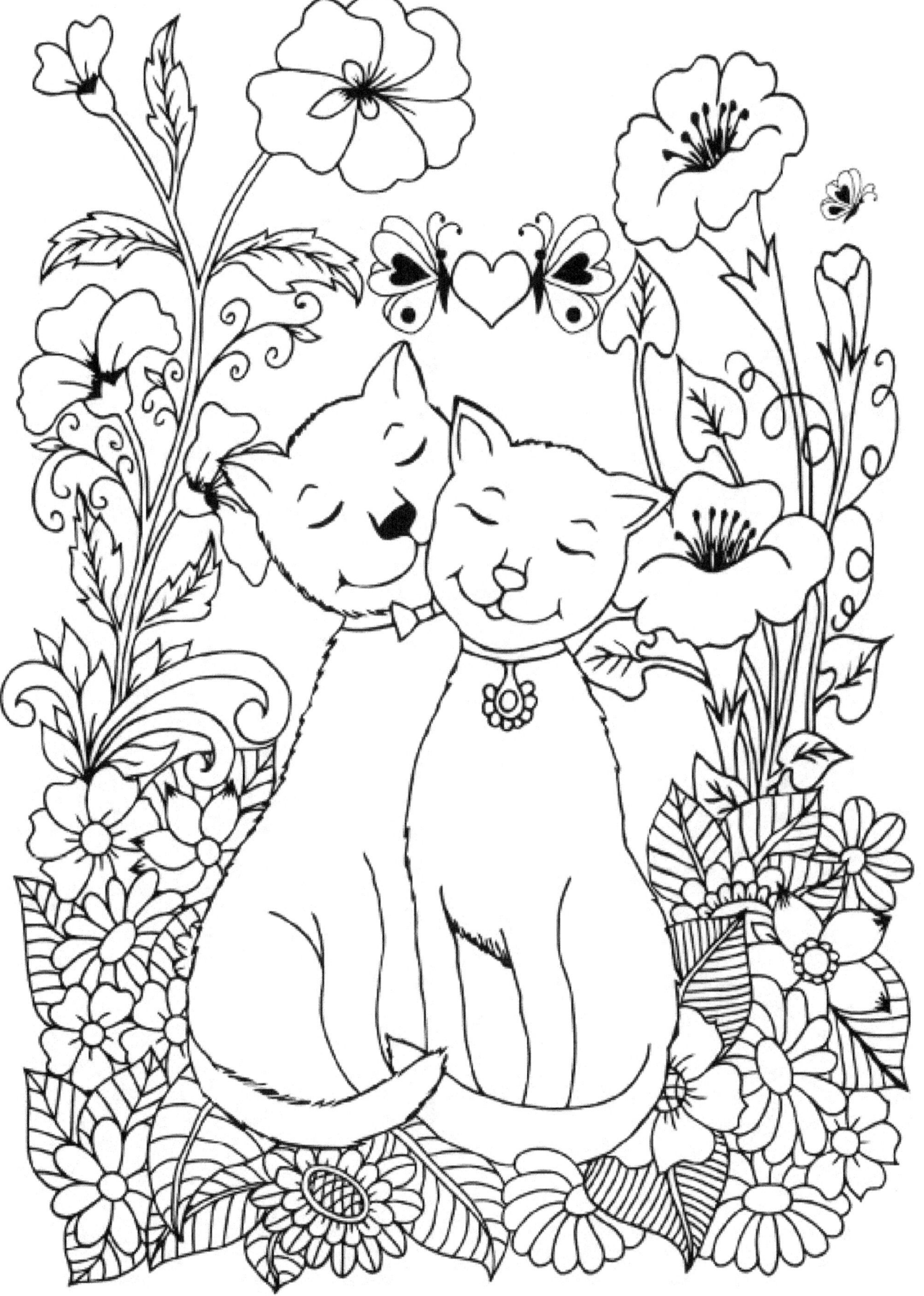

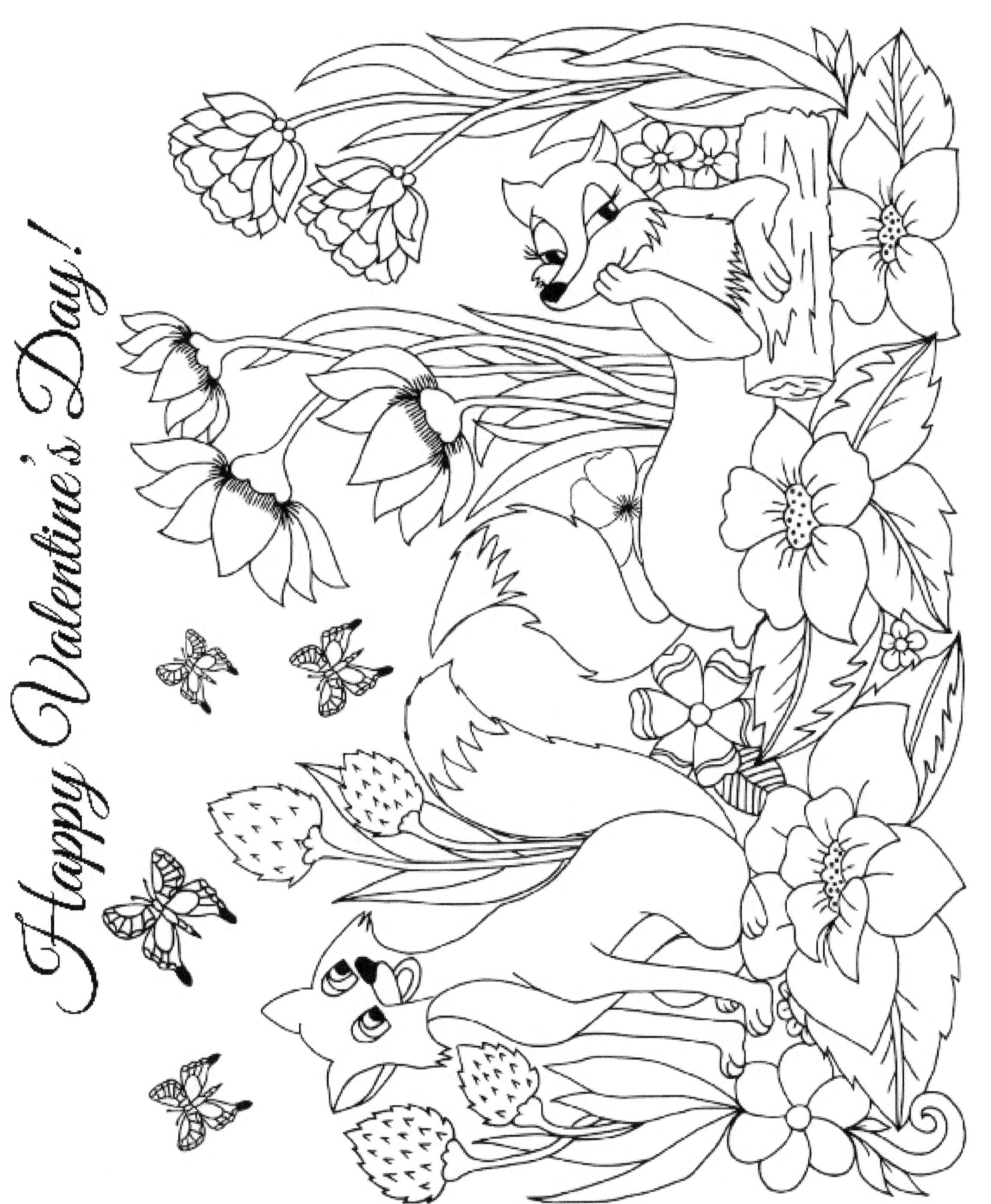

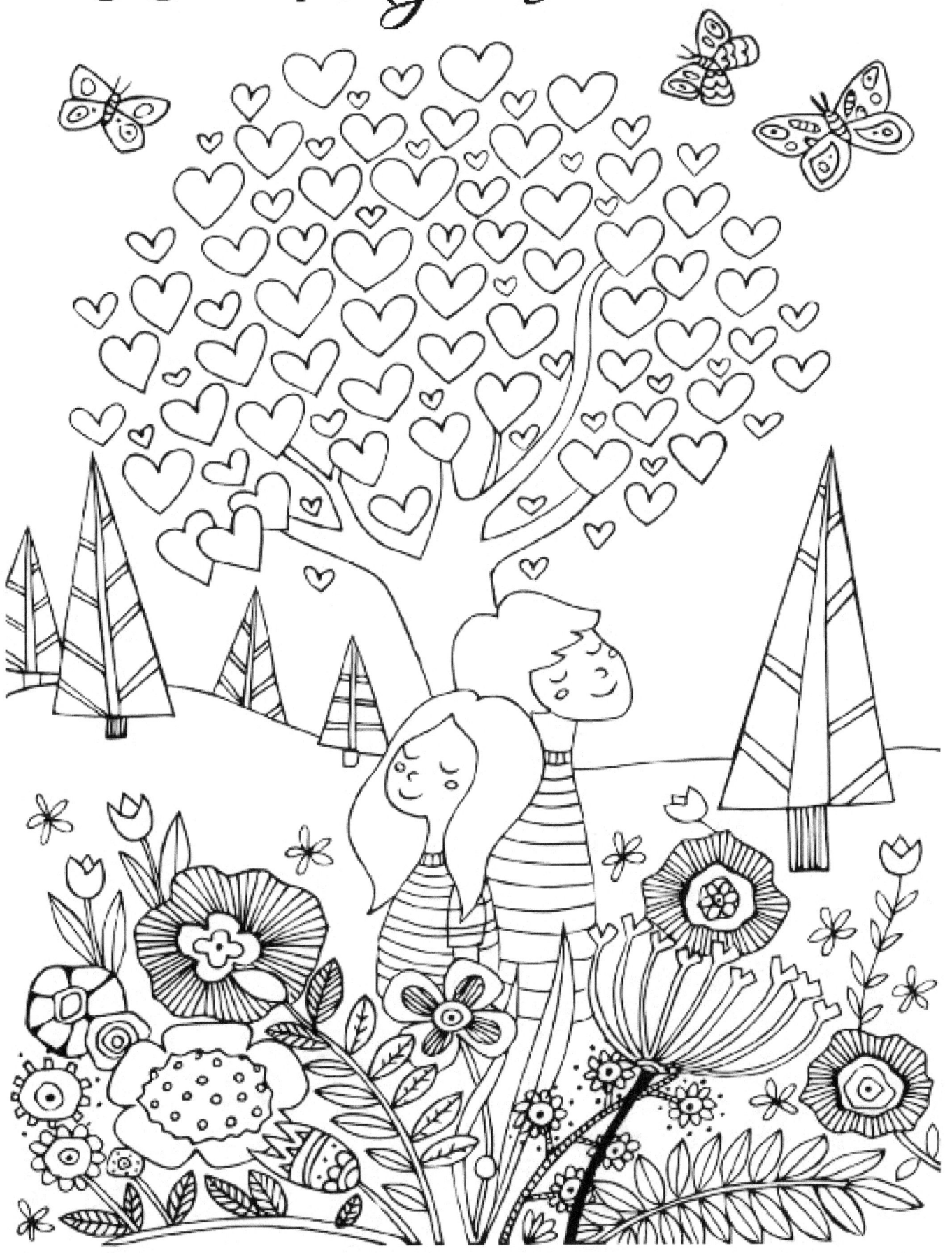

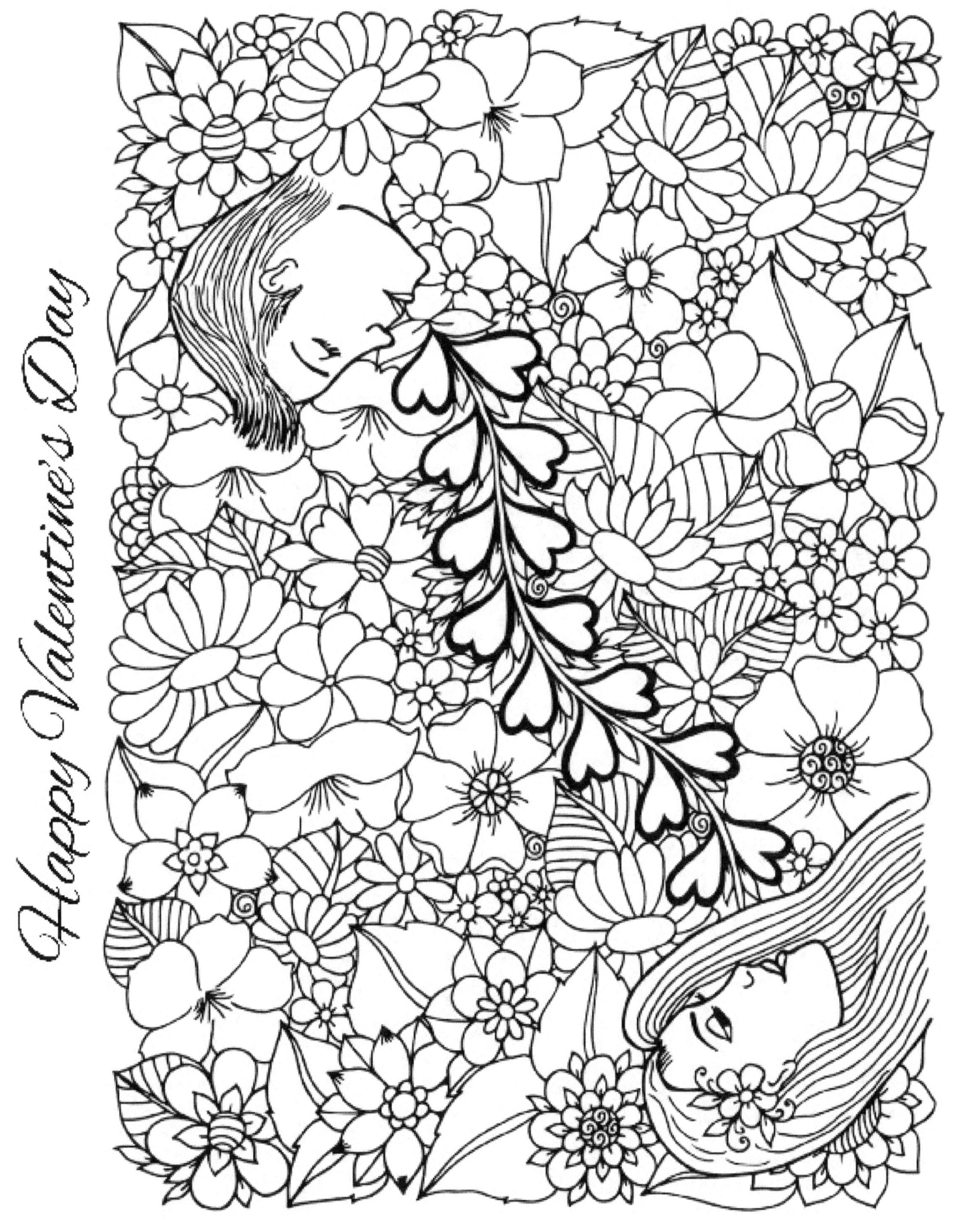

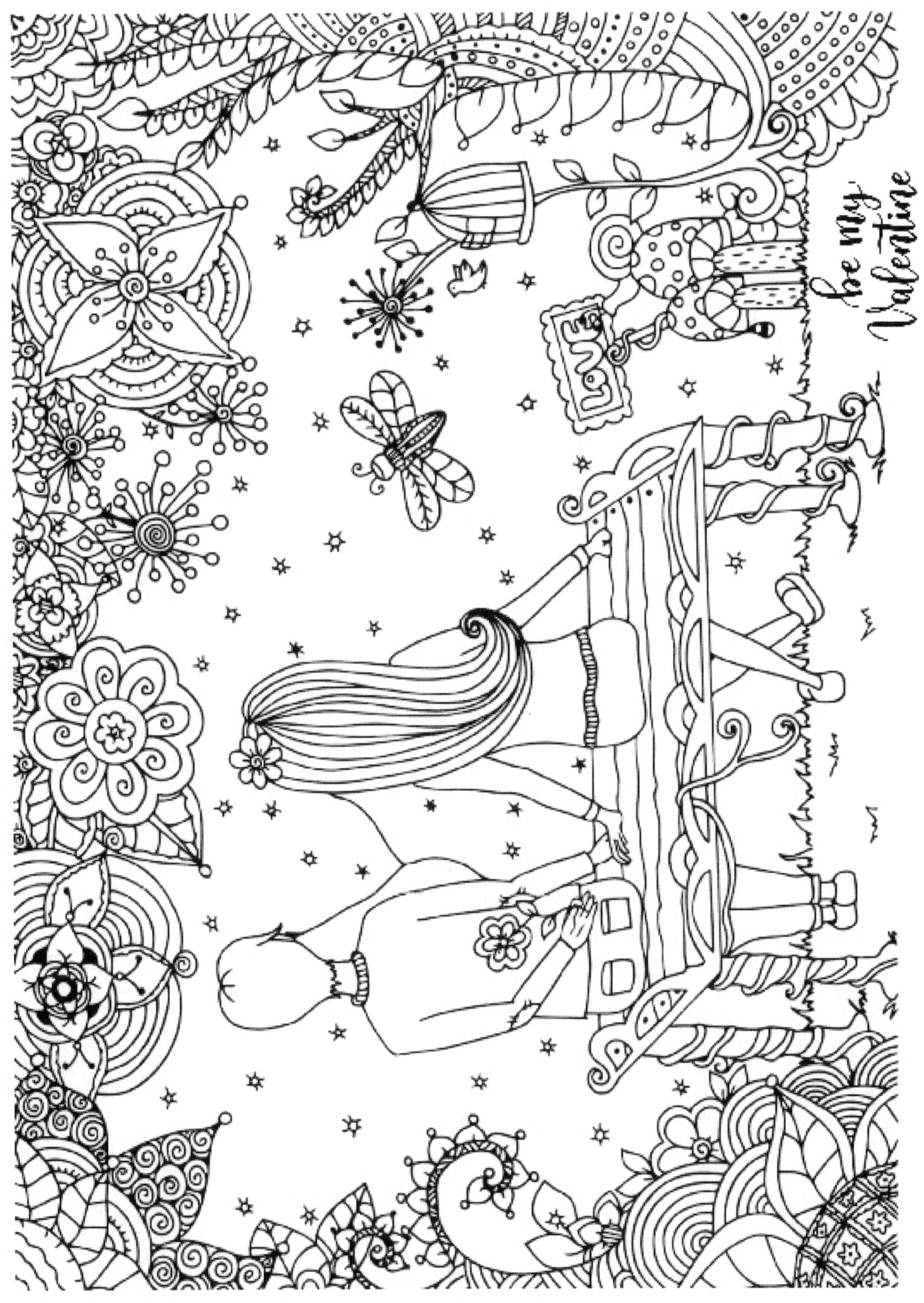

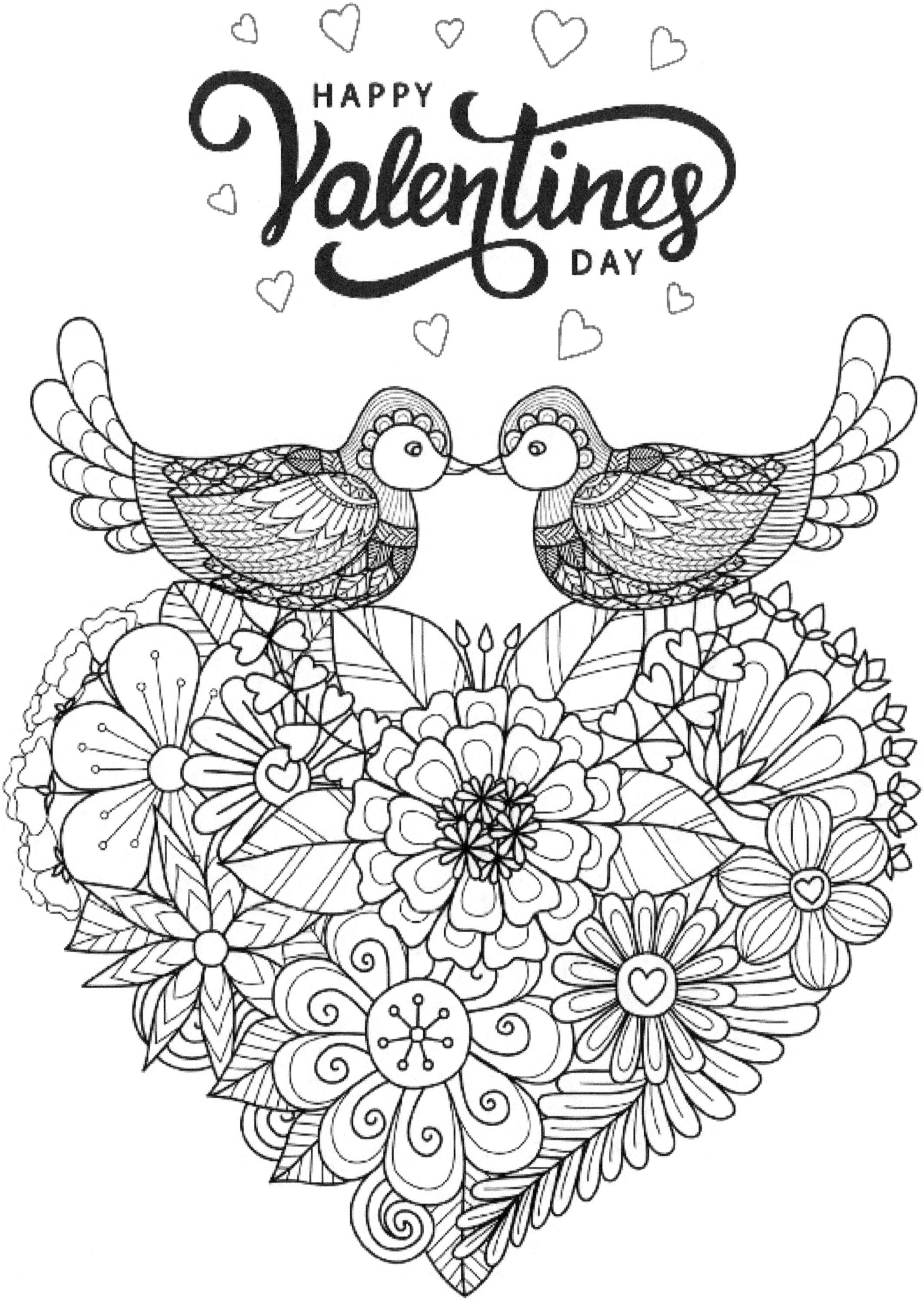

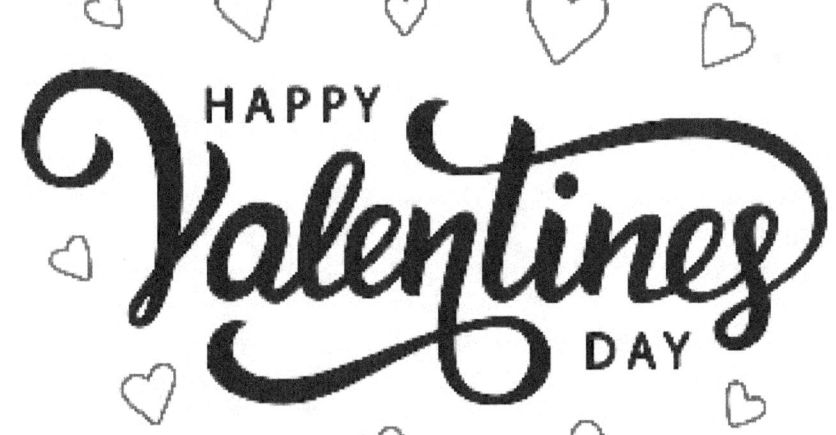

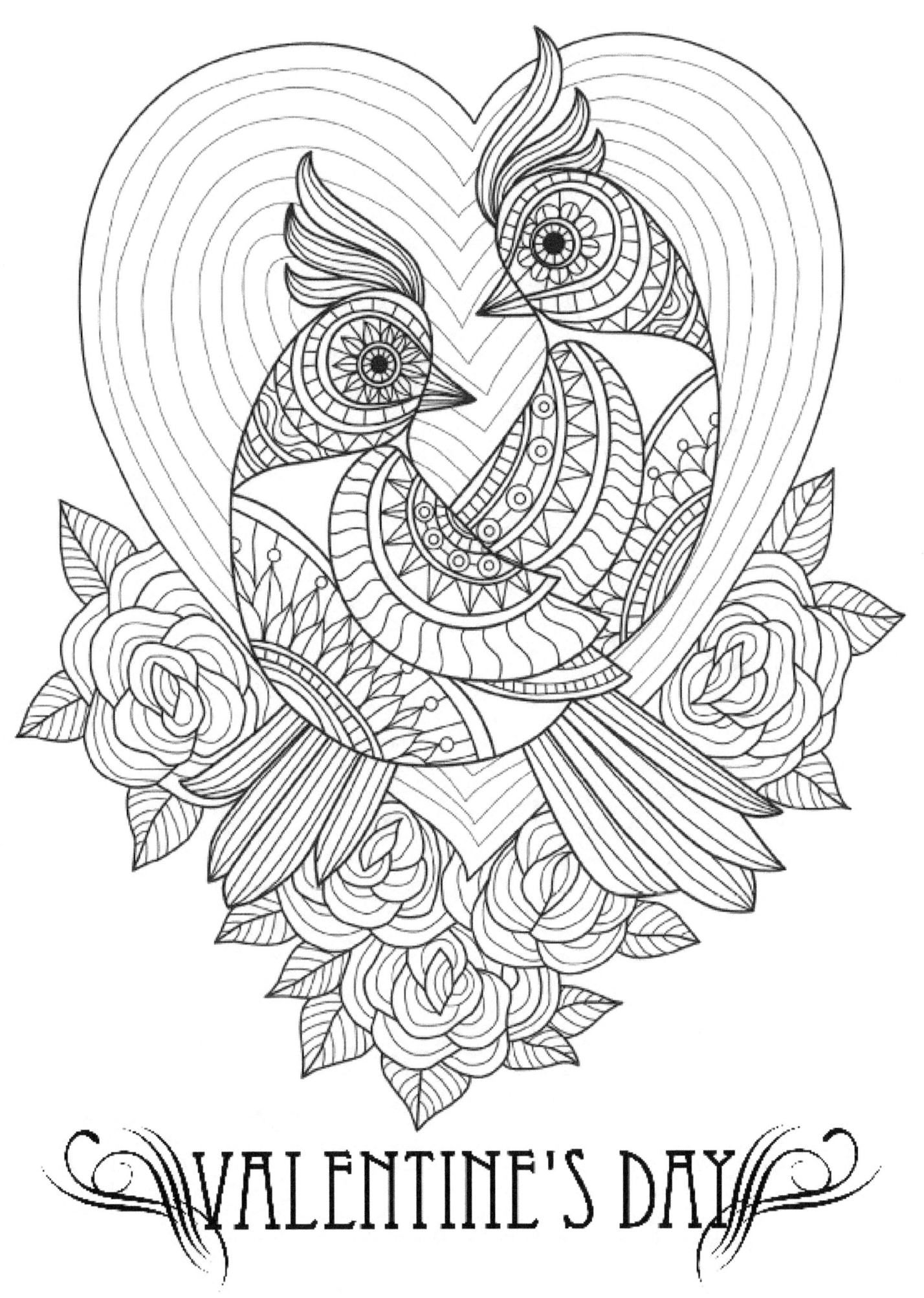

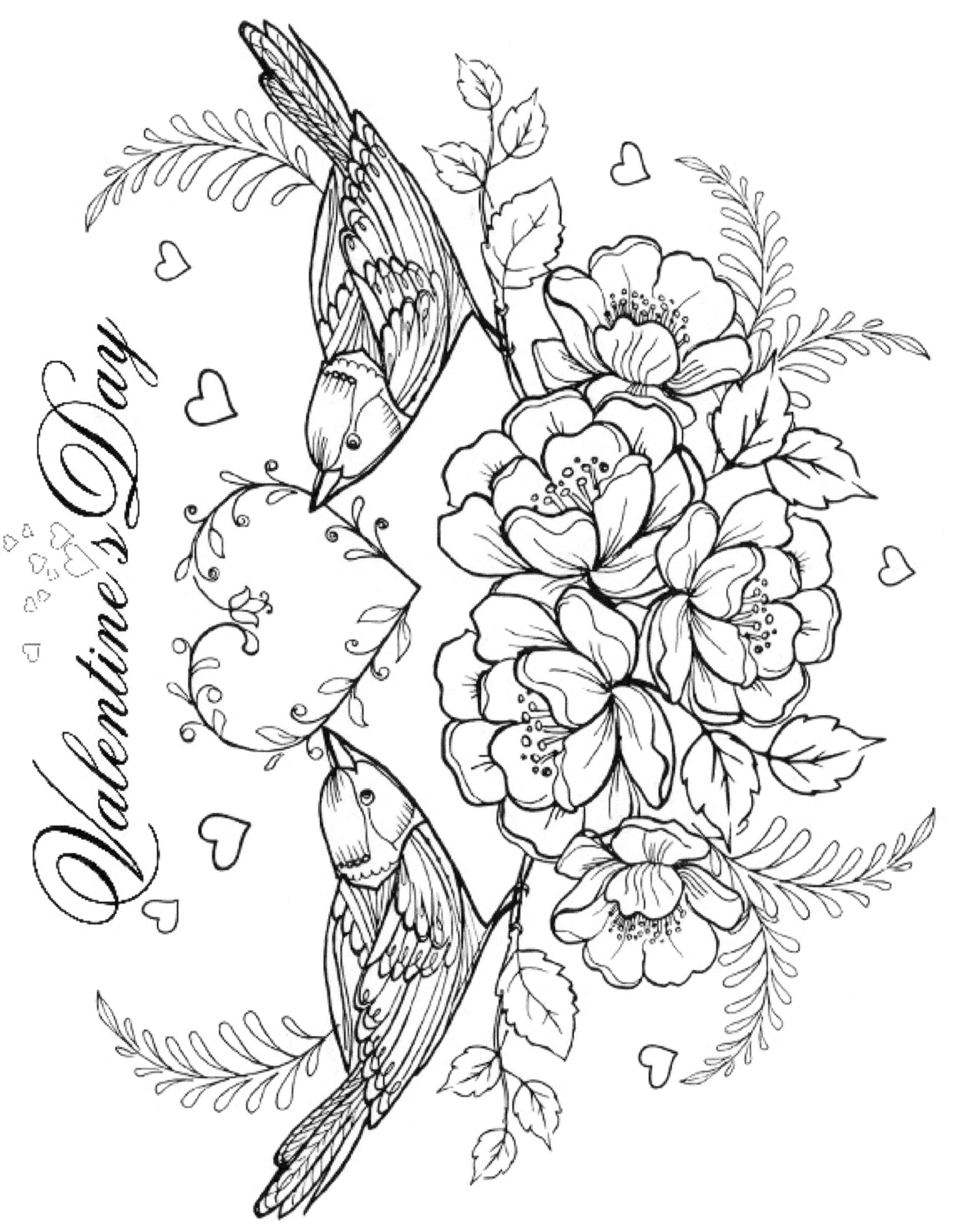

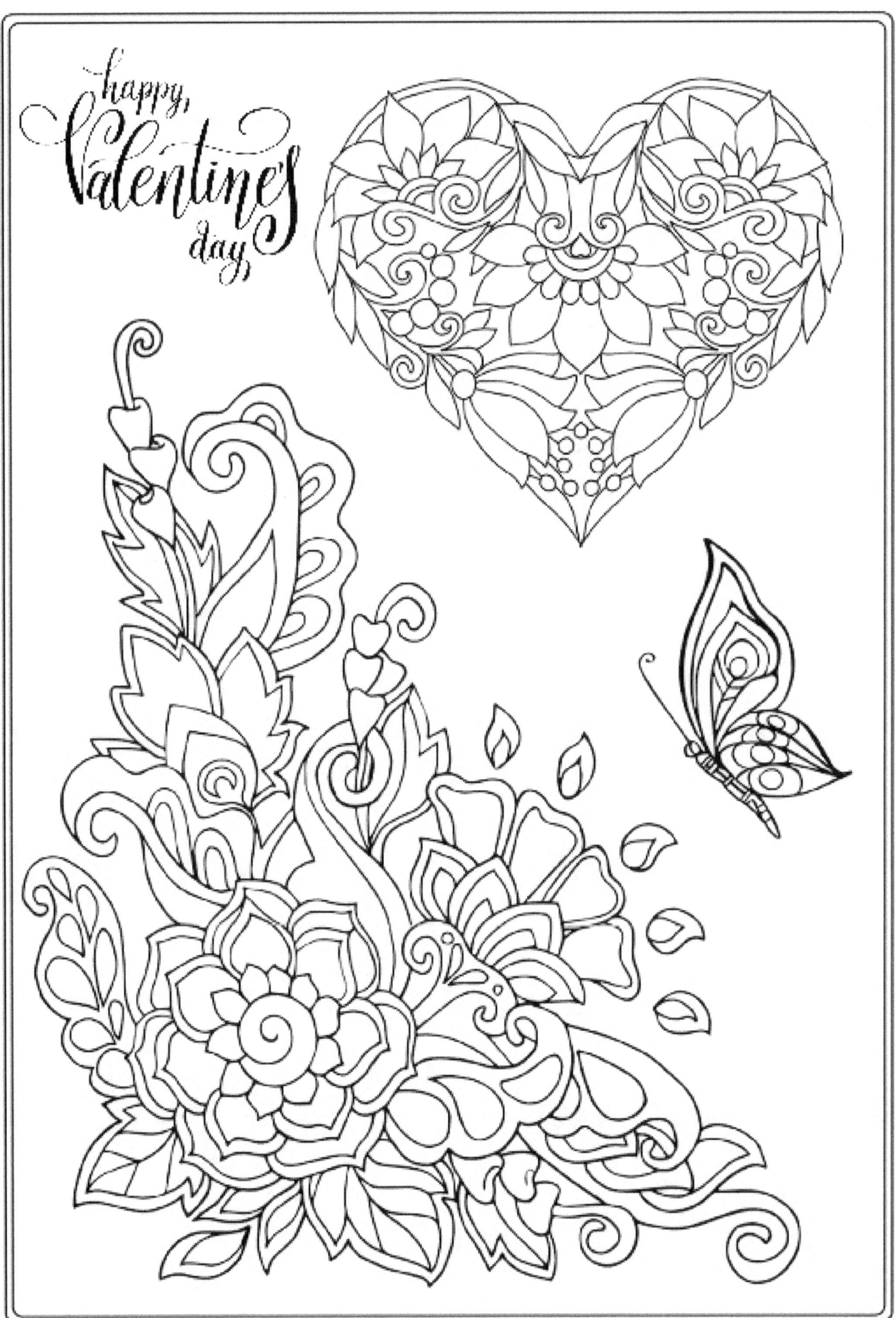

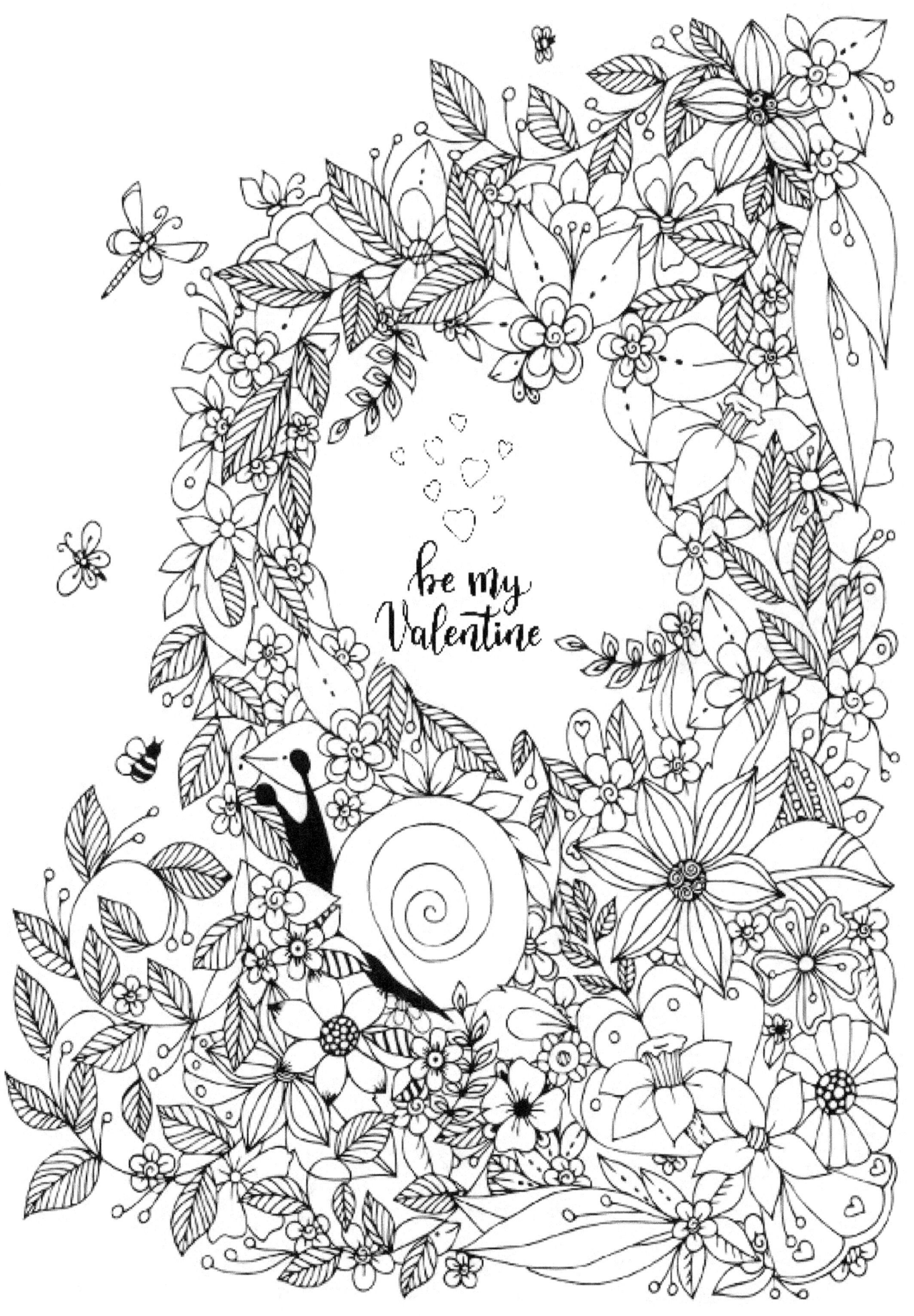

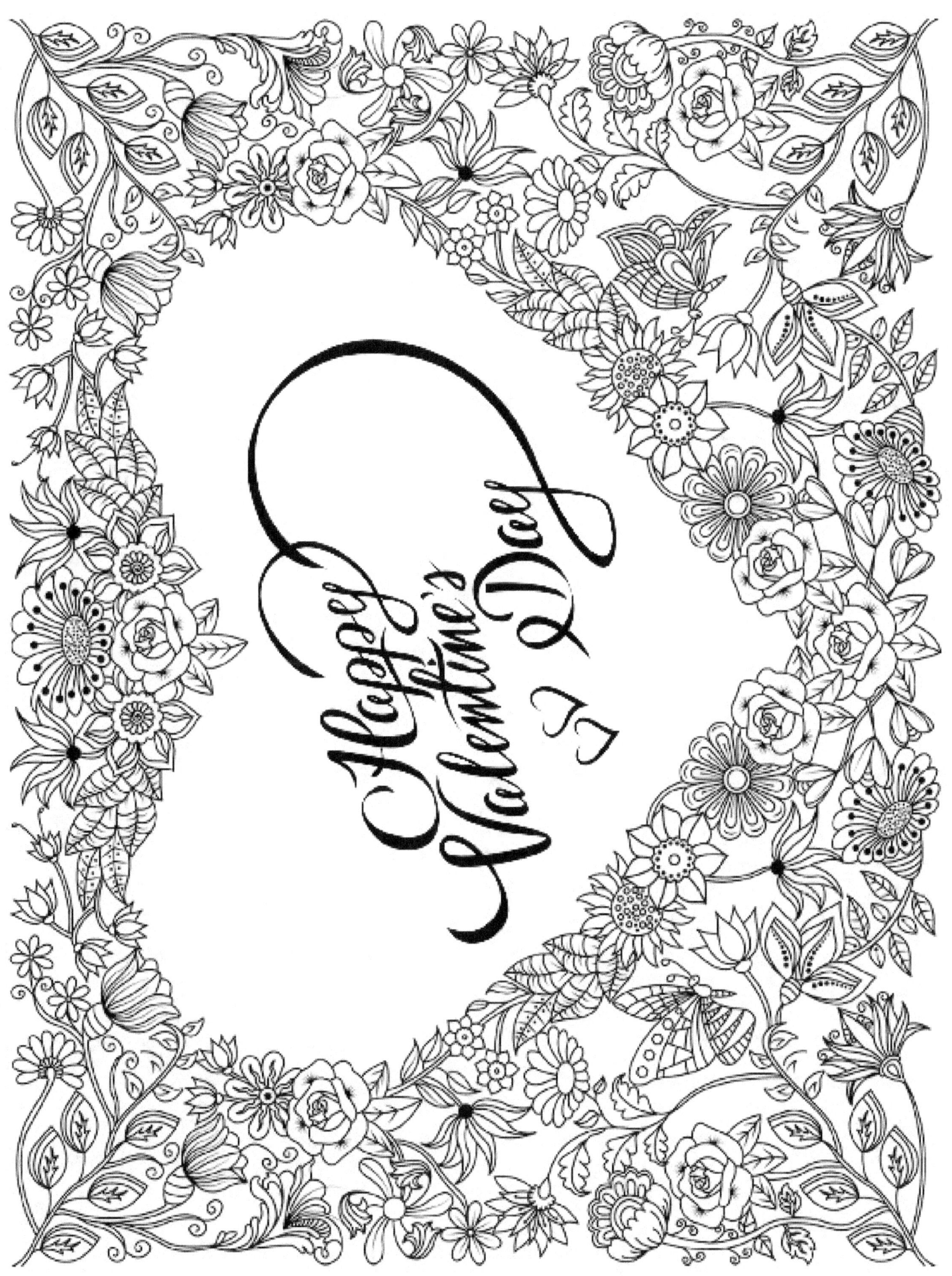

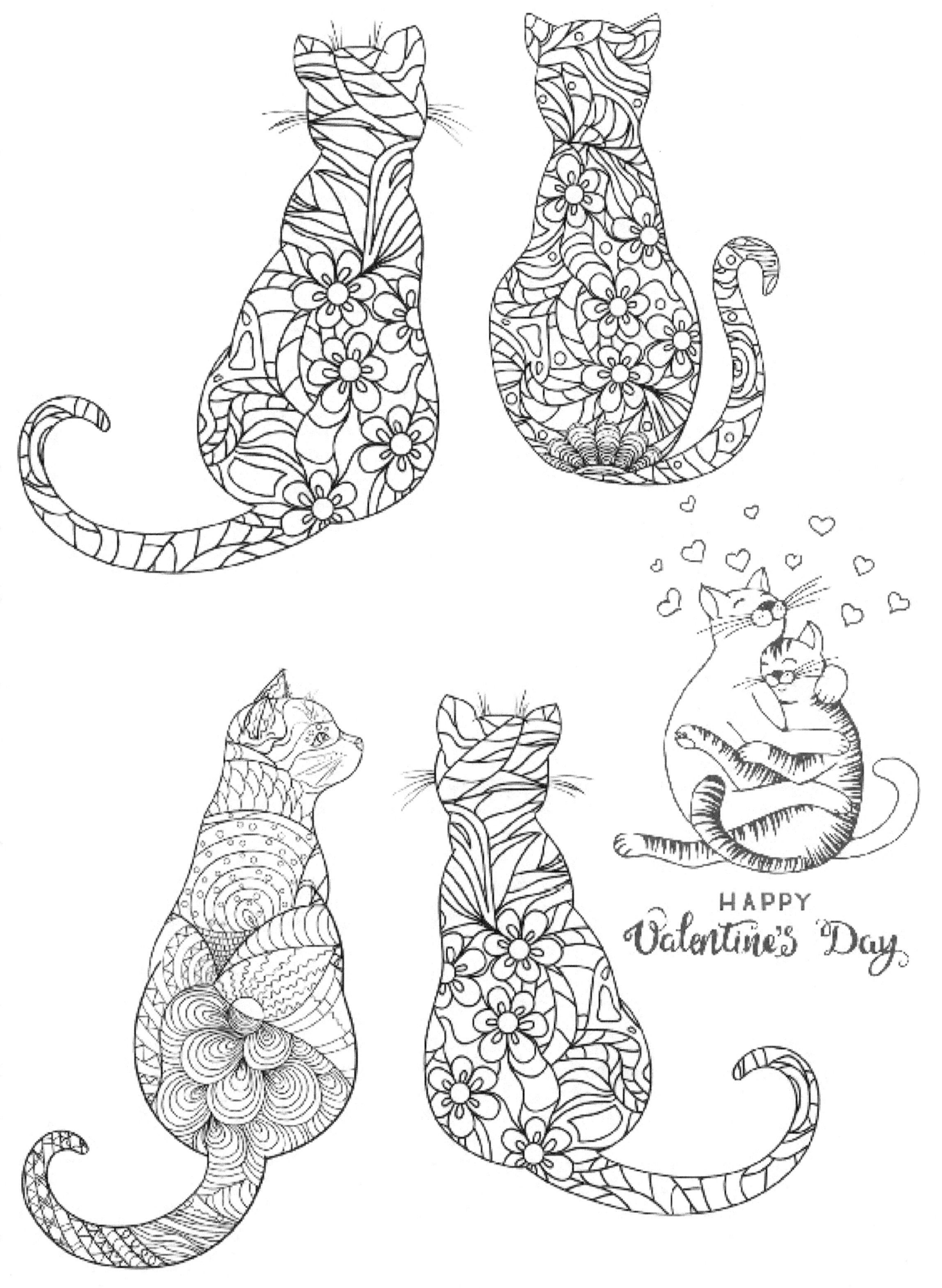

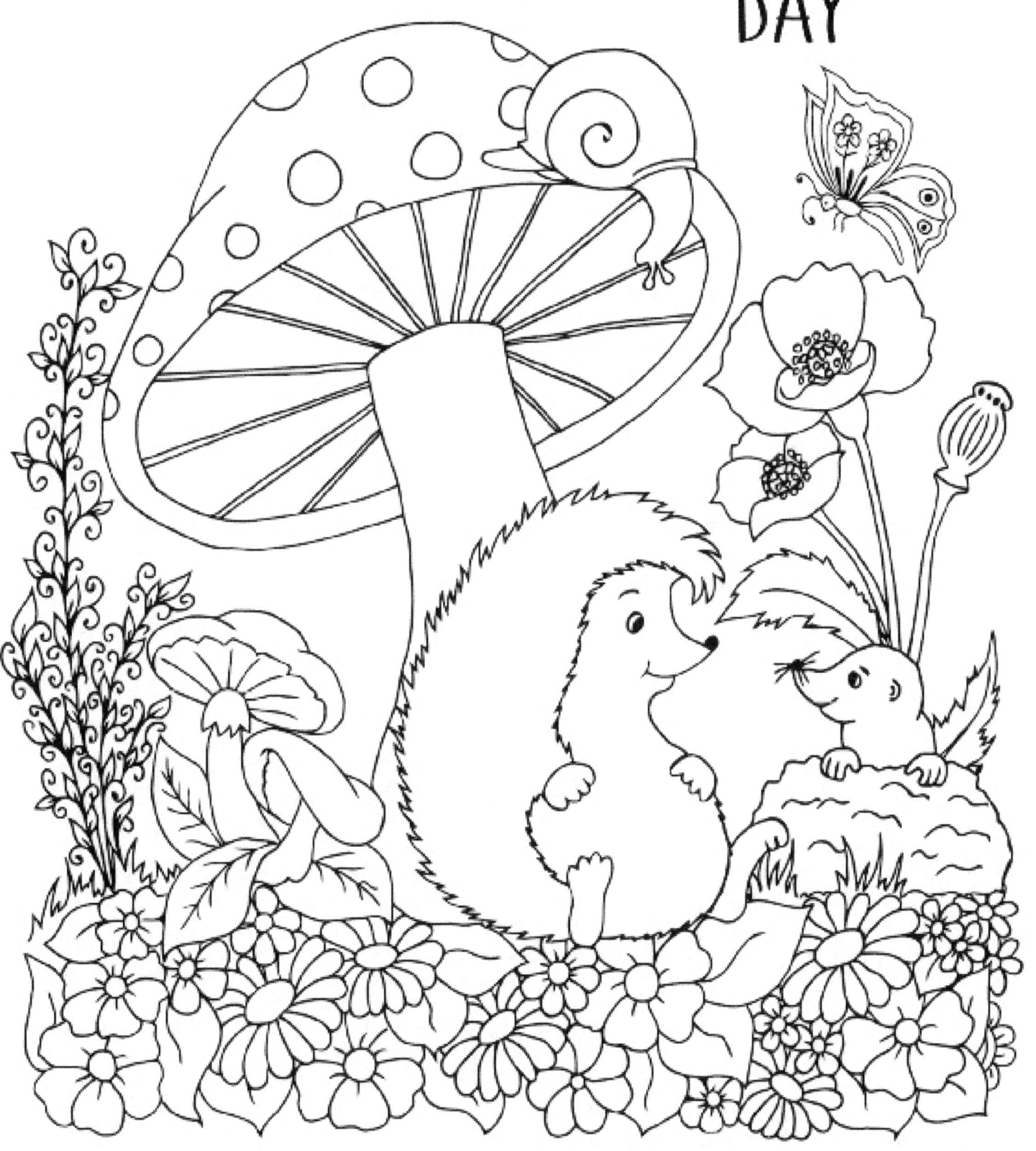

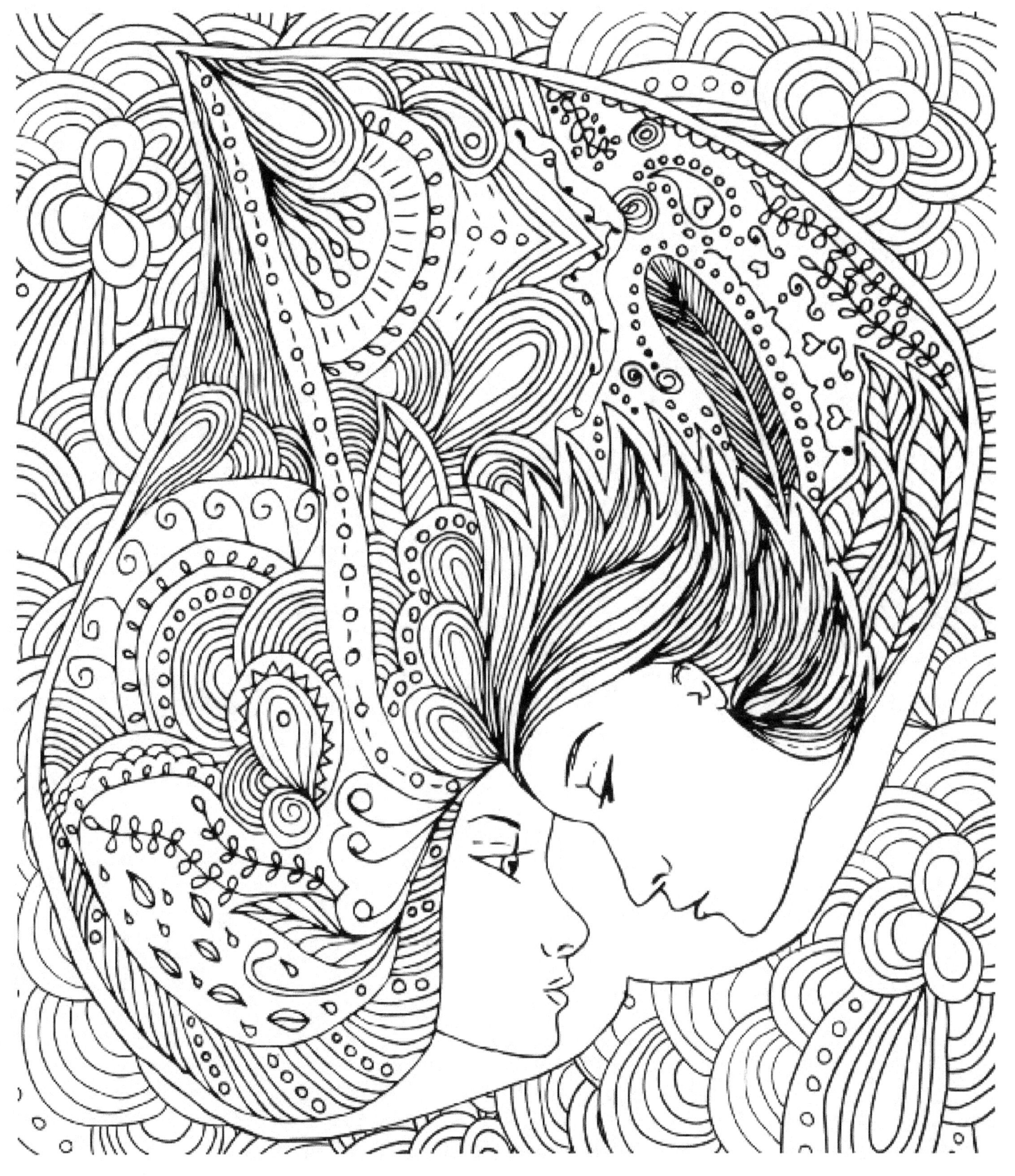

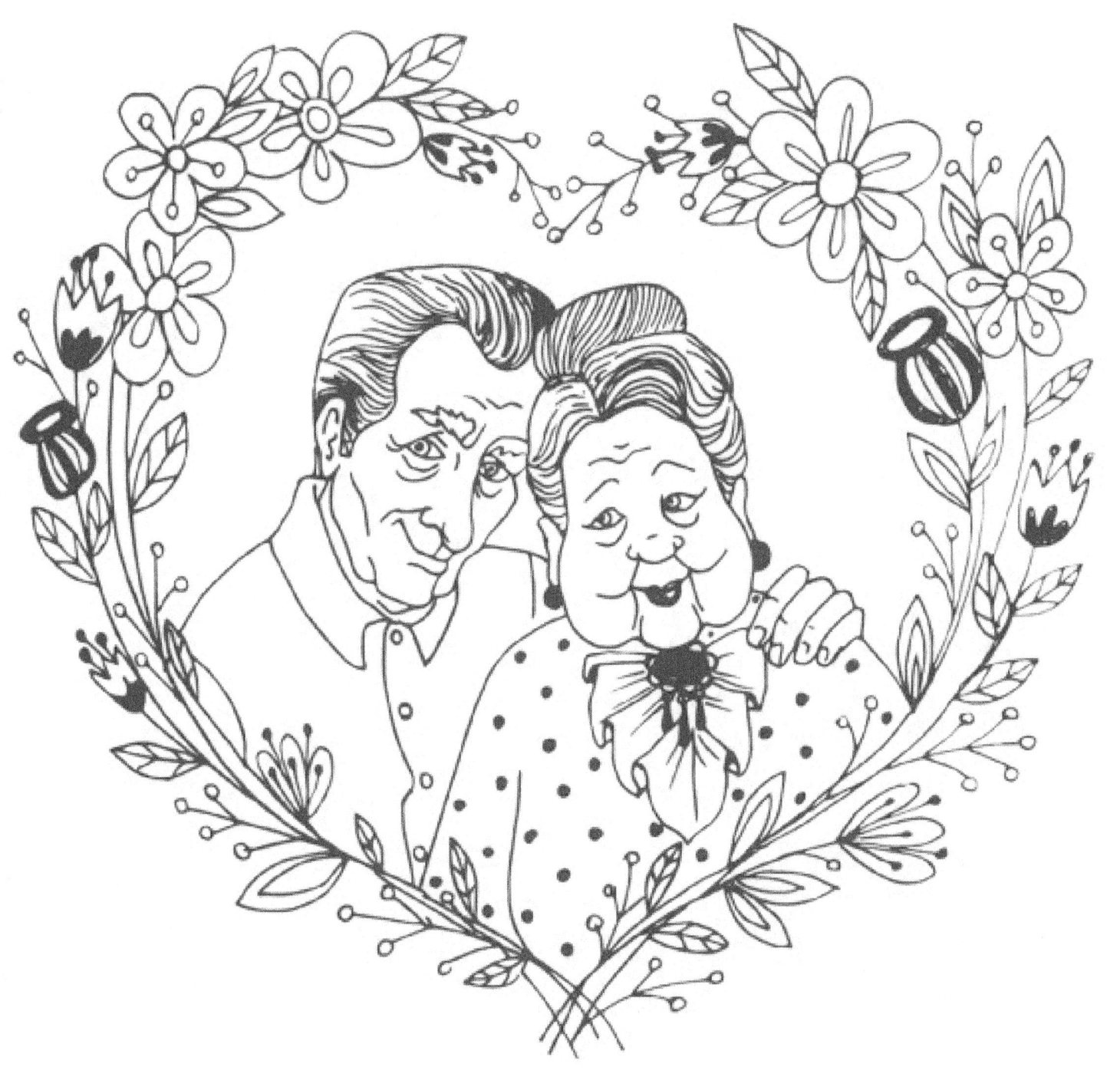

HAPPY
Valentine's Day

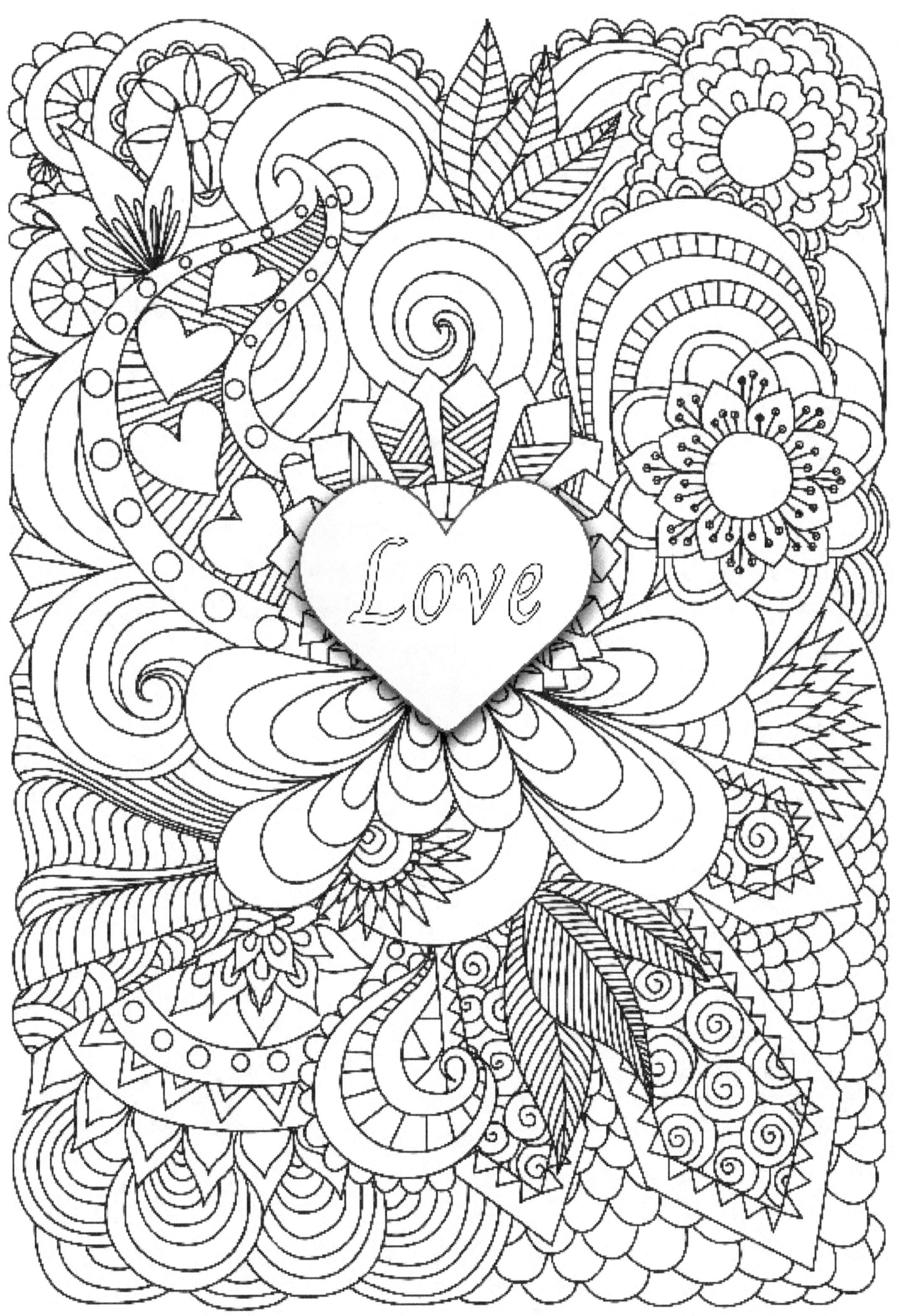

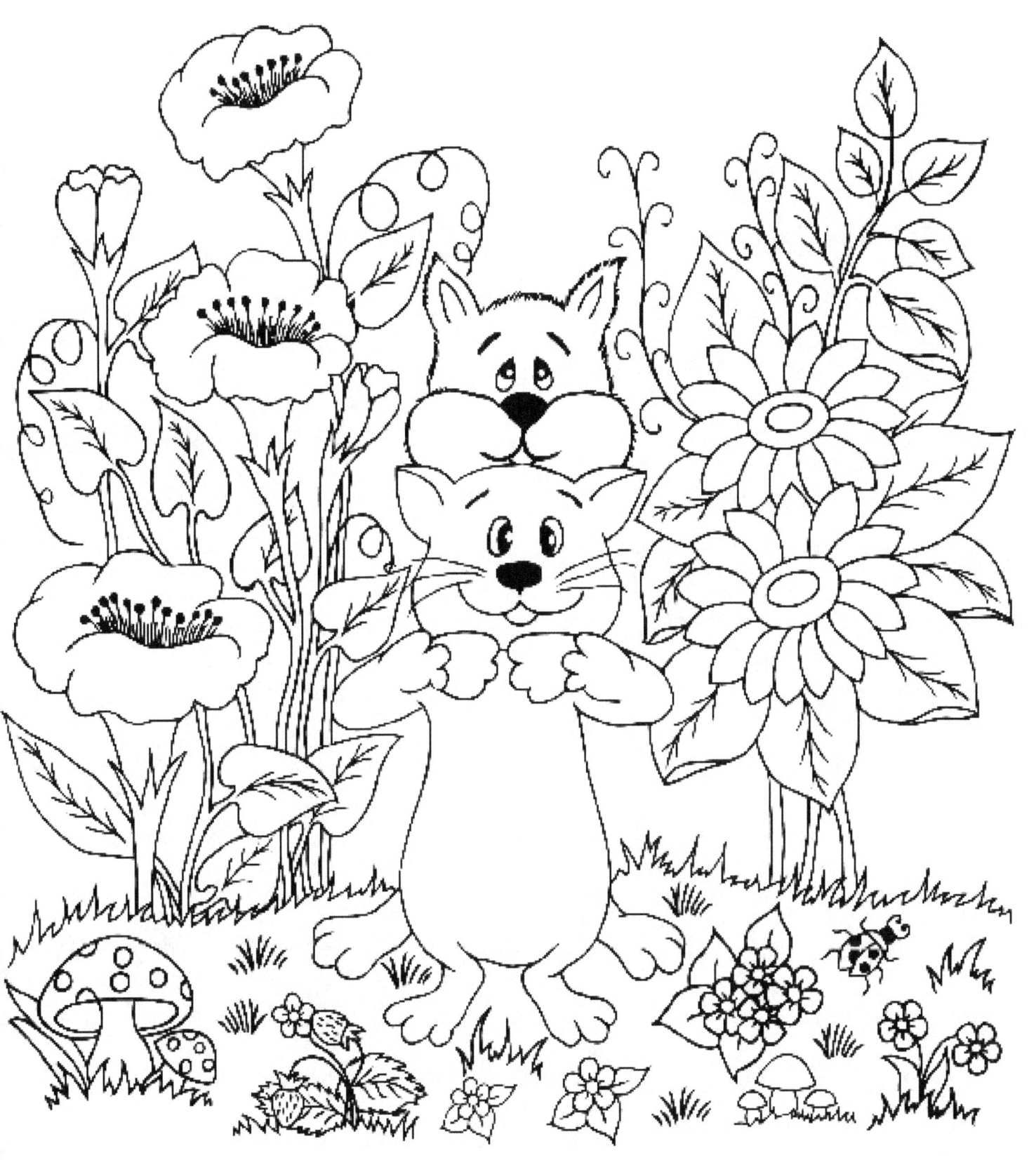

Happy Valentine's Day

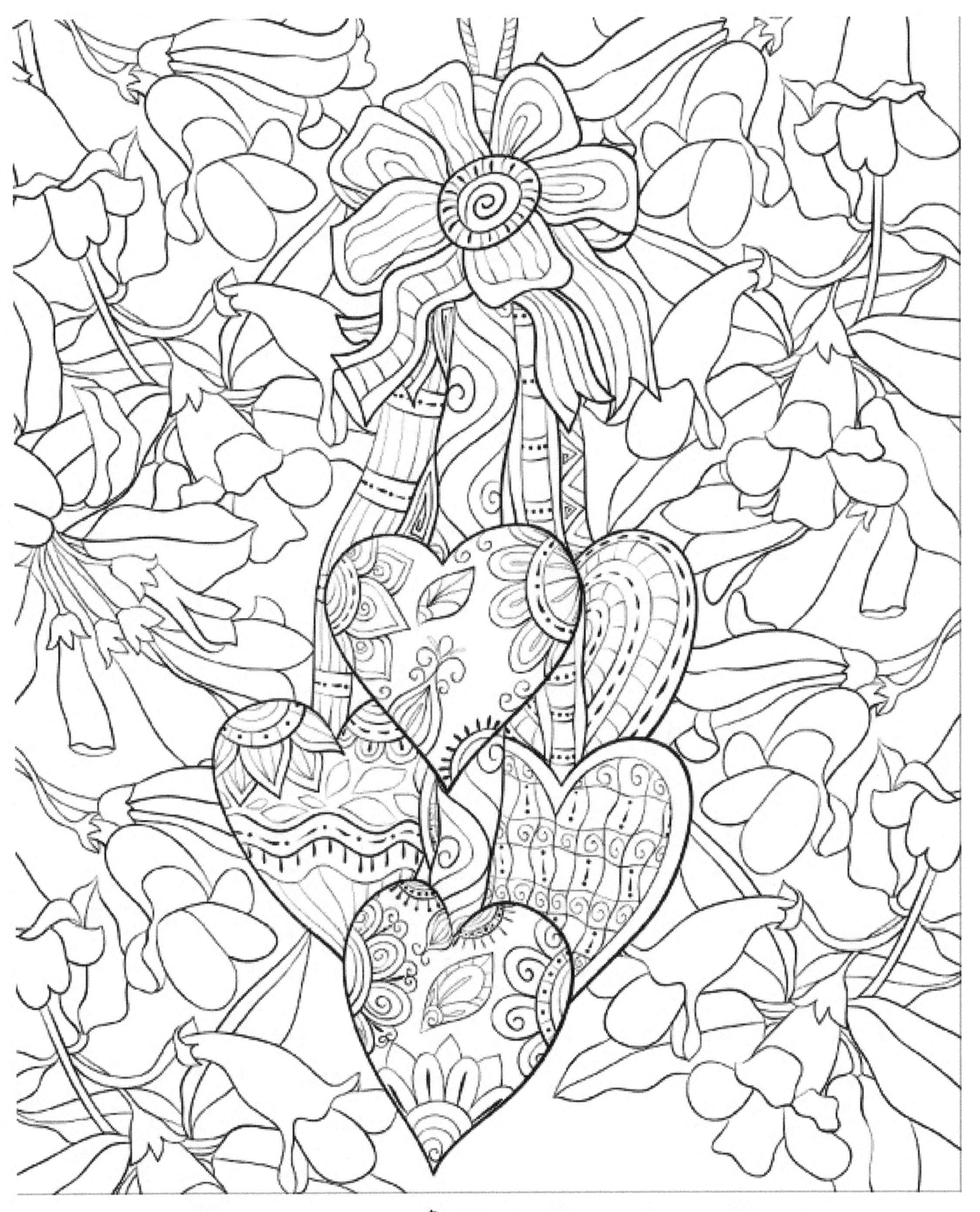
Happy Valentine's Day

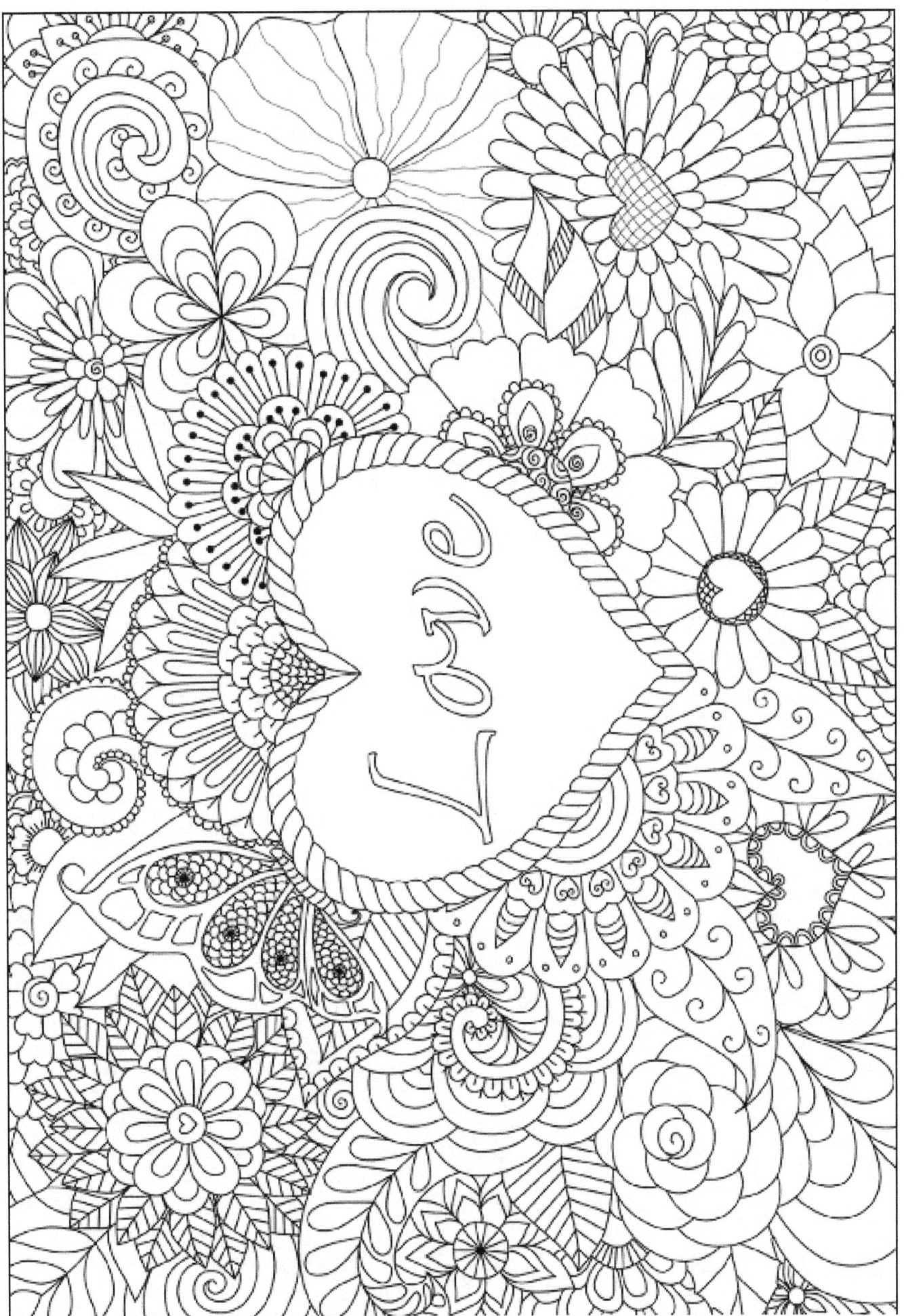

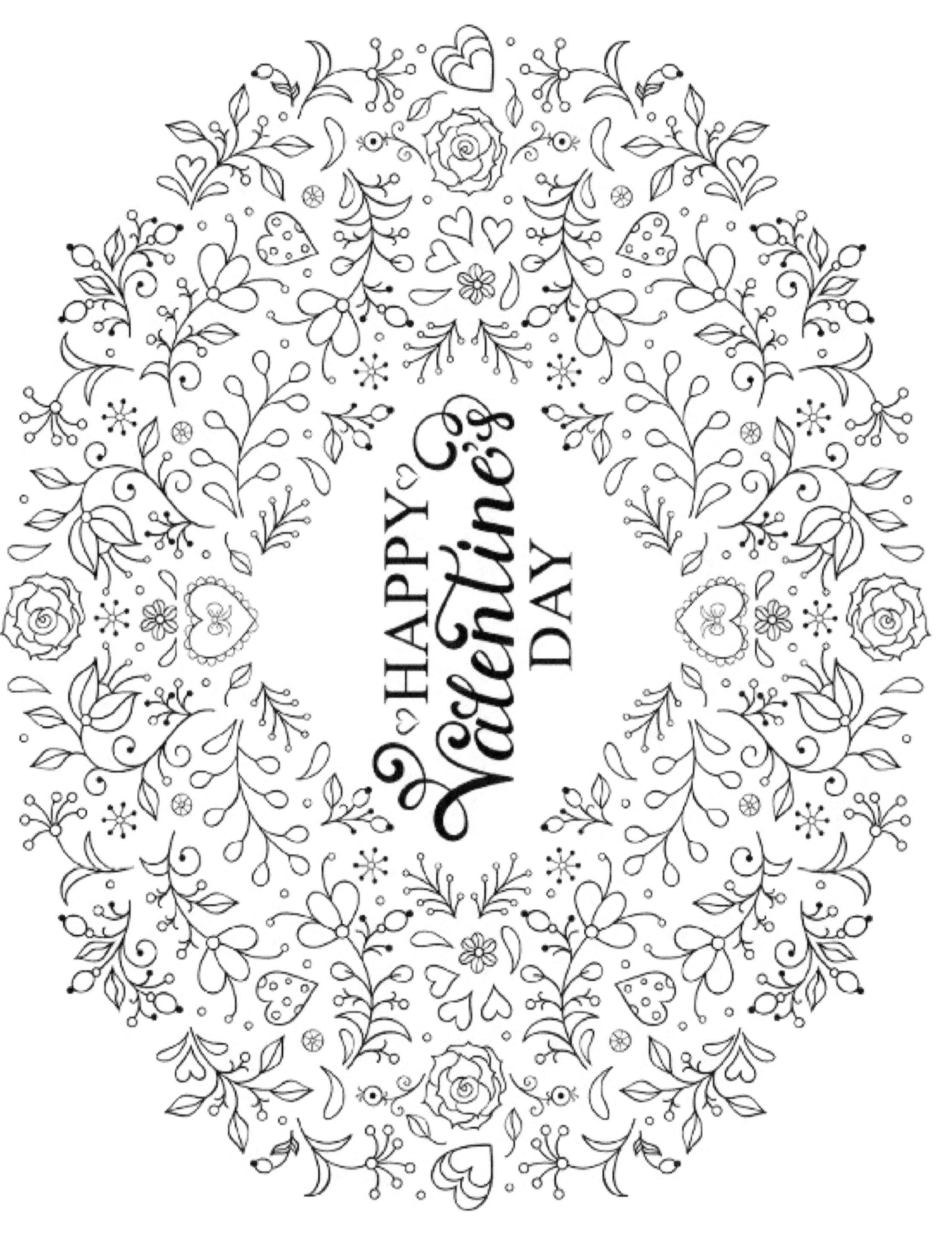

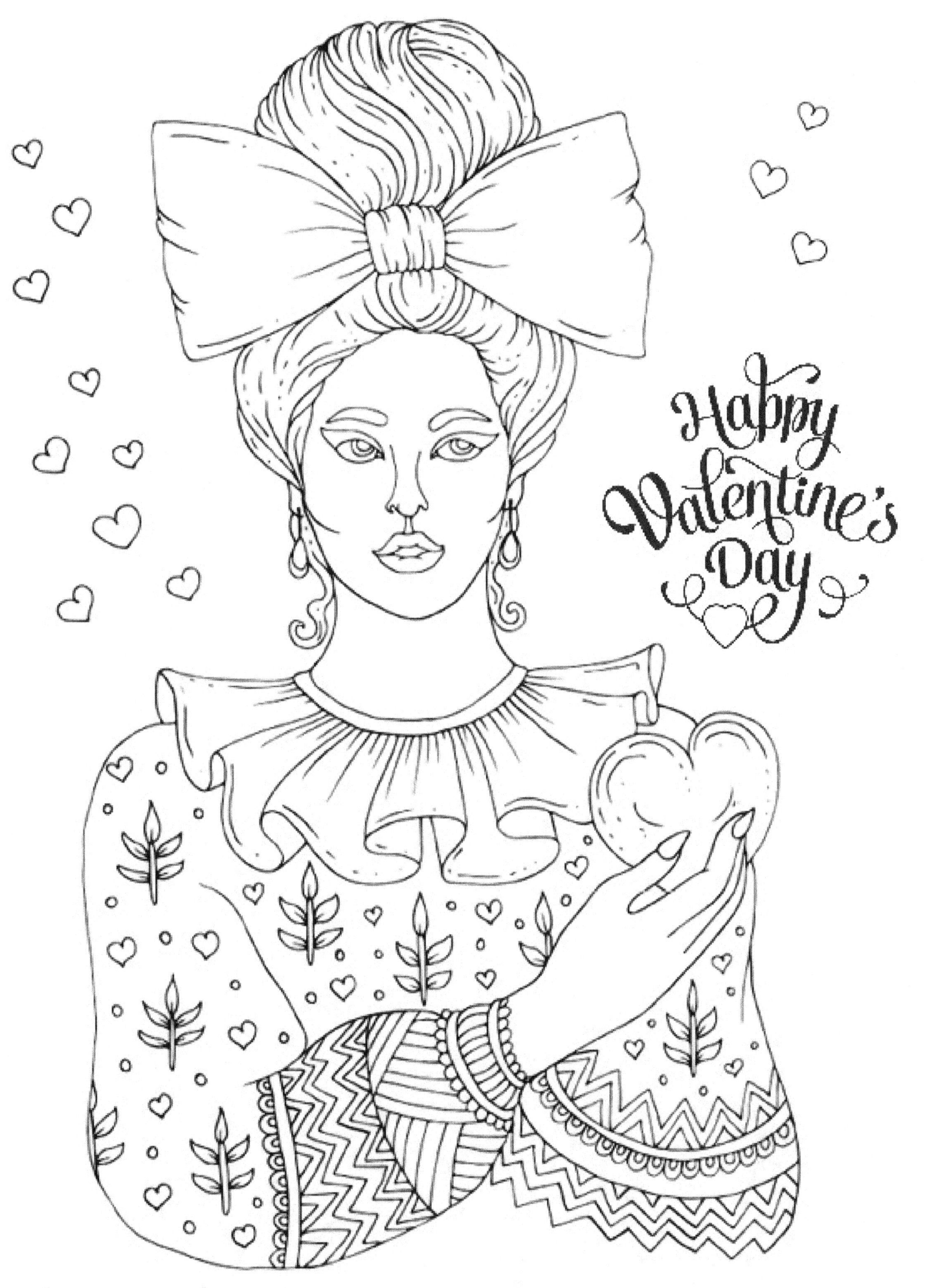

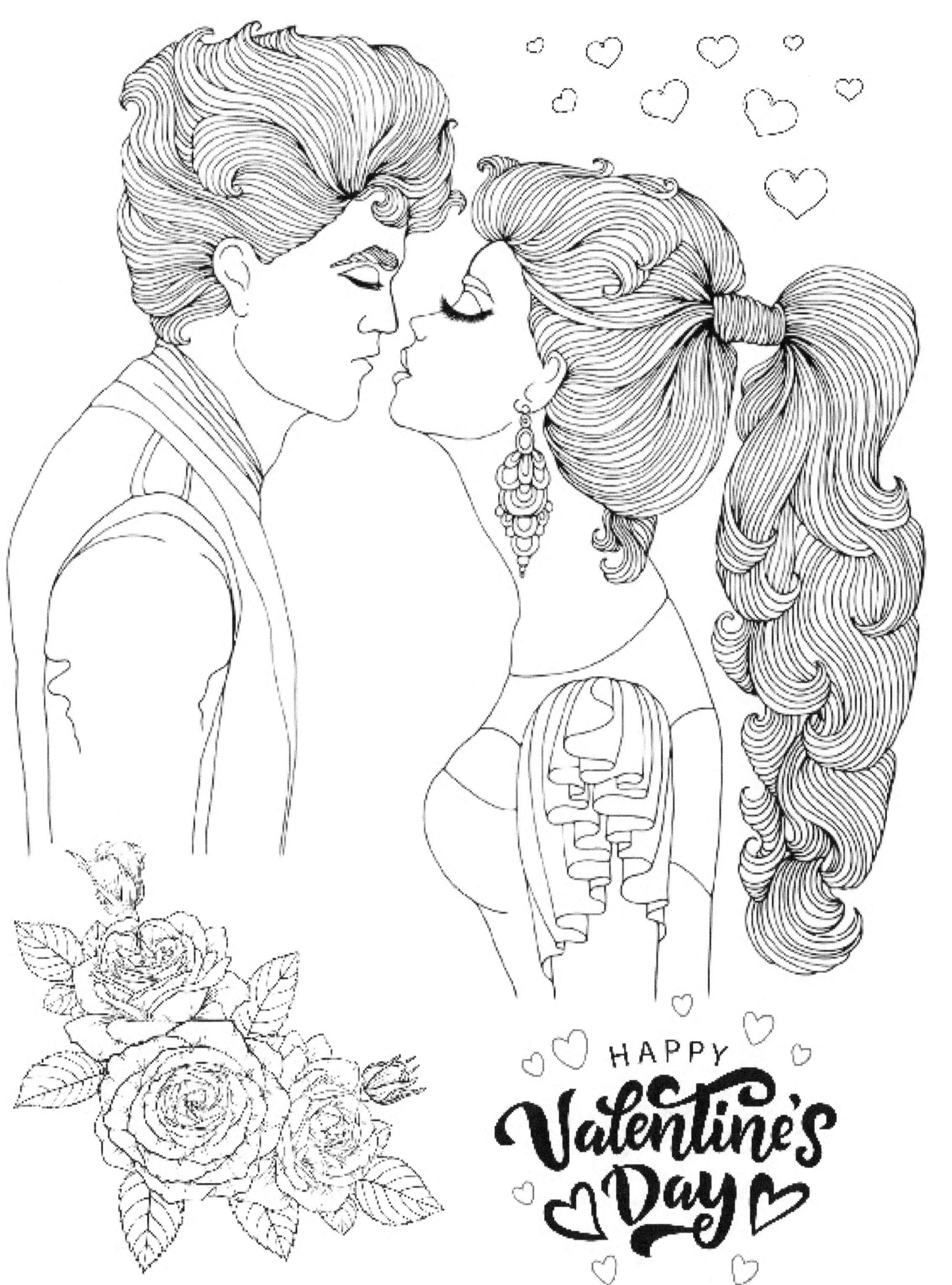

HAPPY **Valentine's** DAY

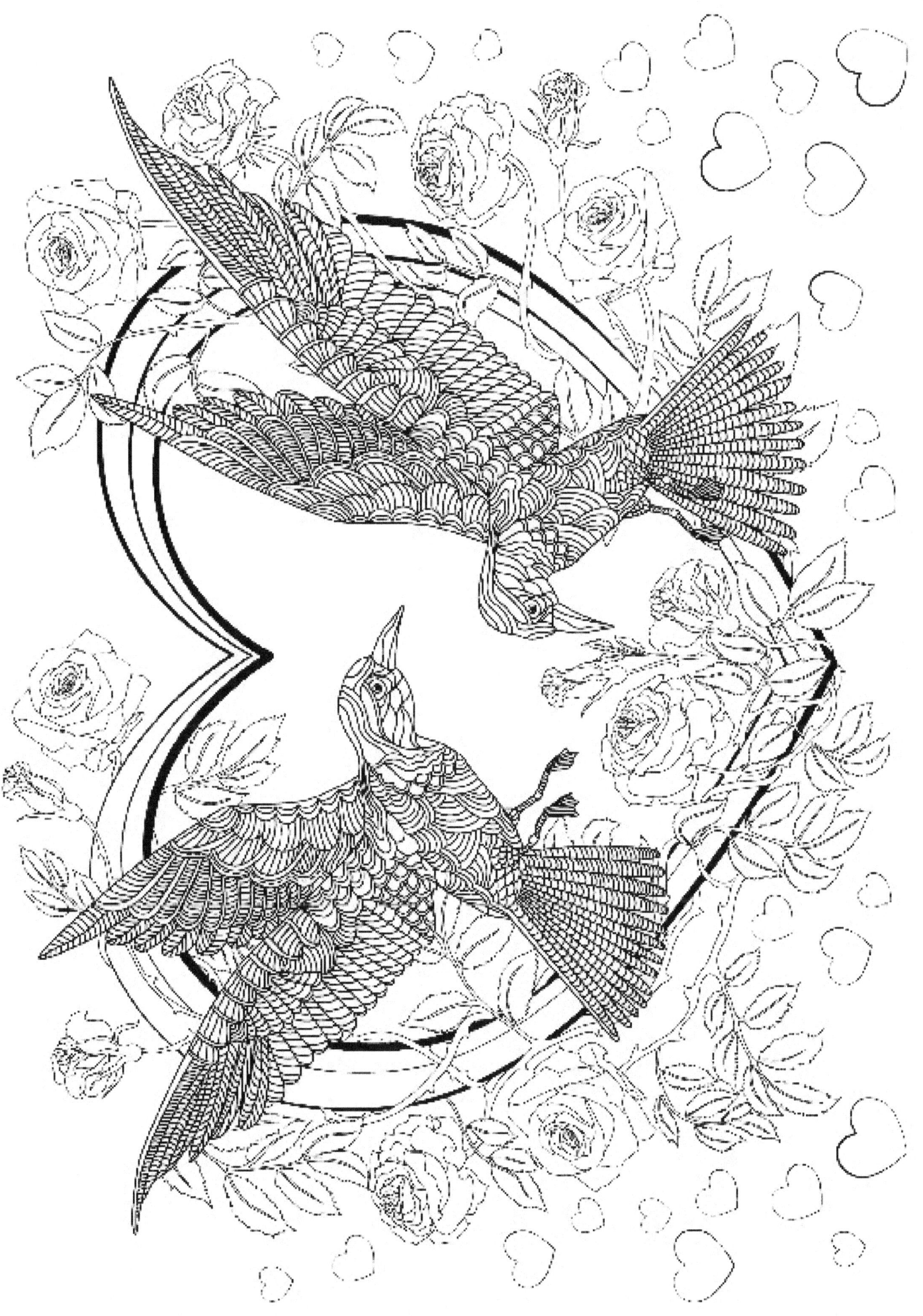

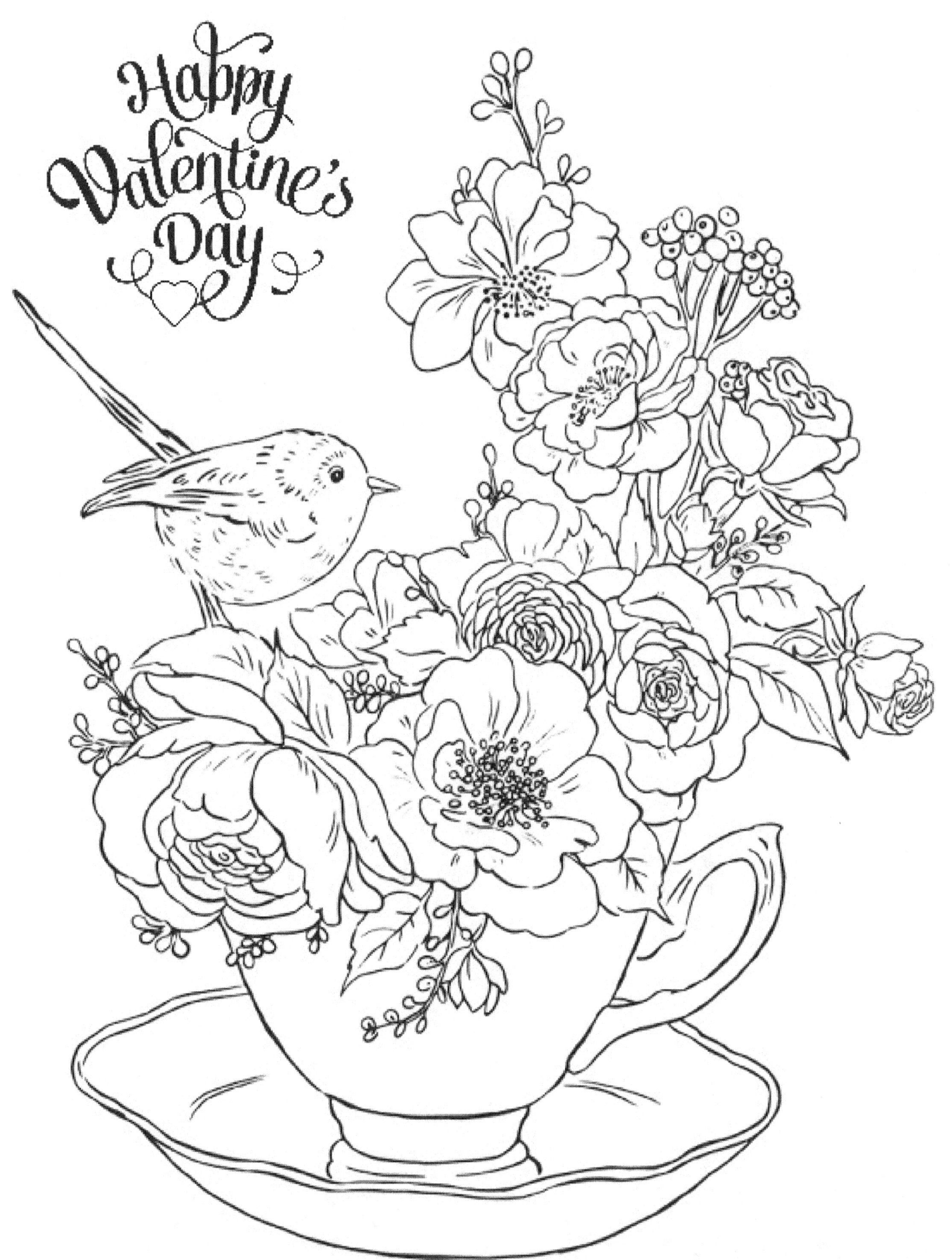

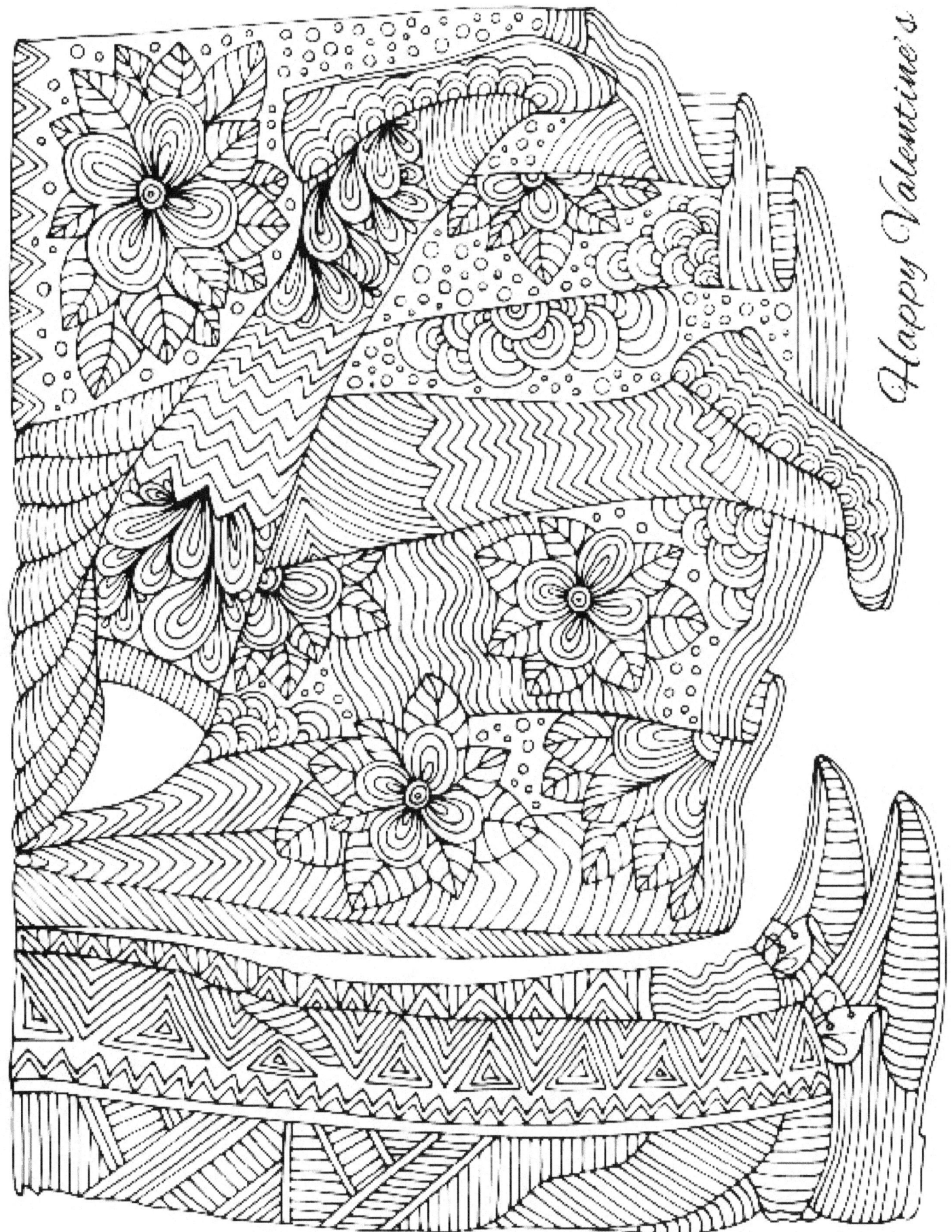

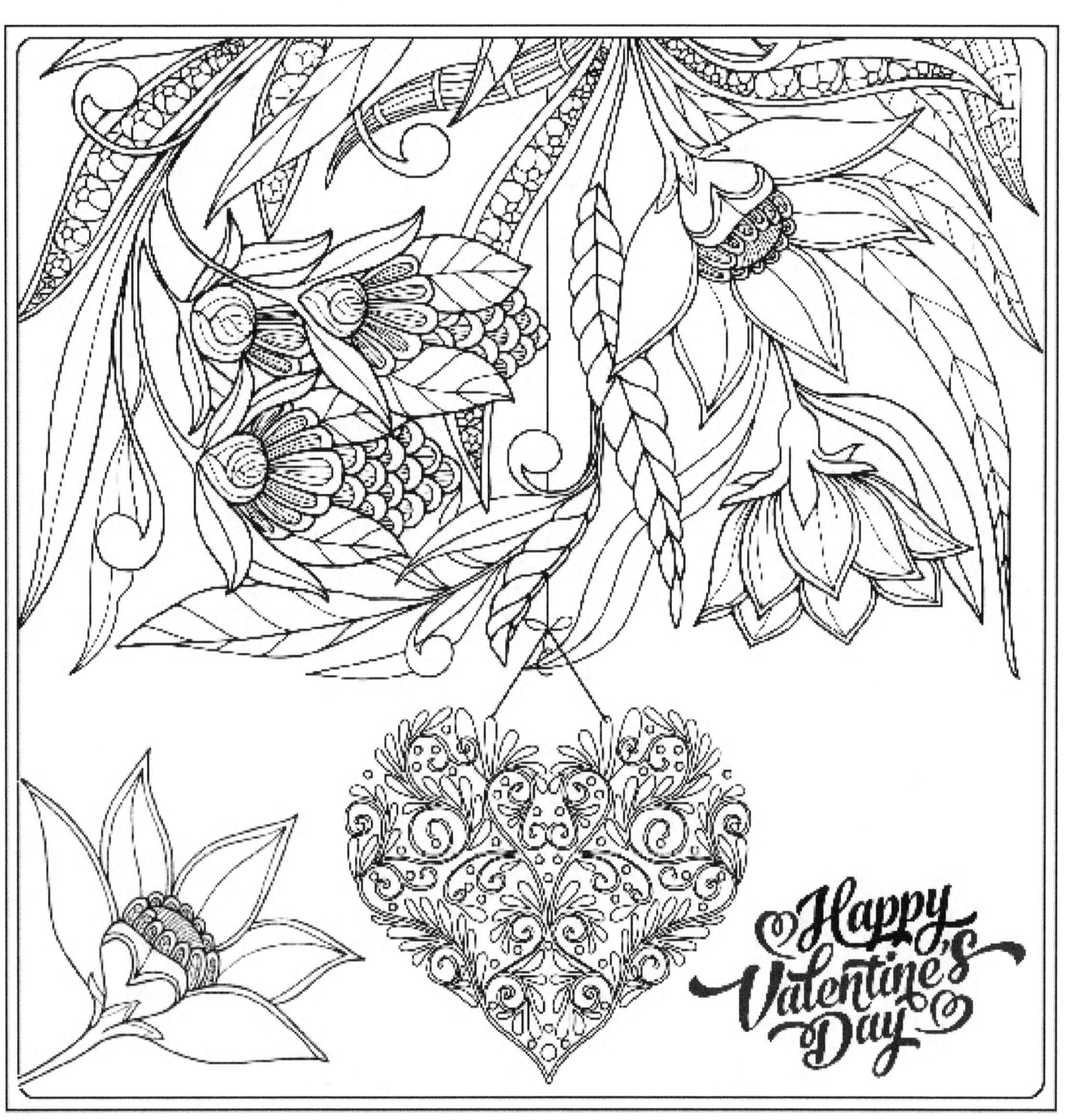

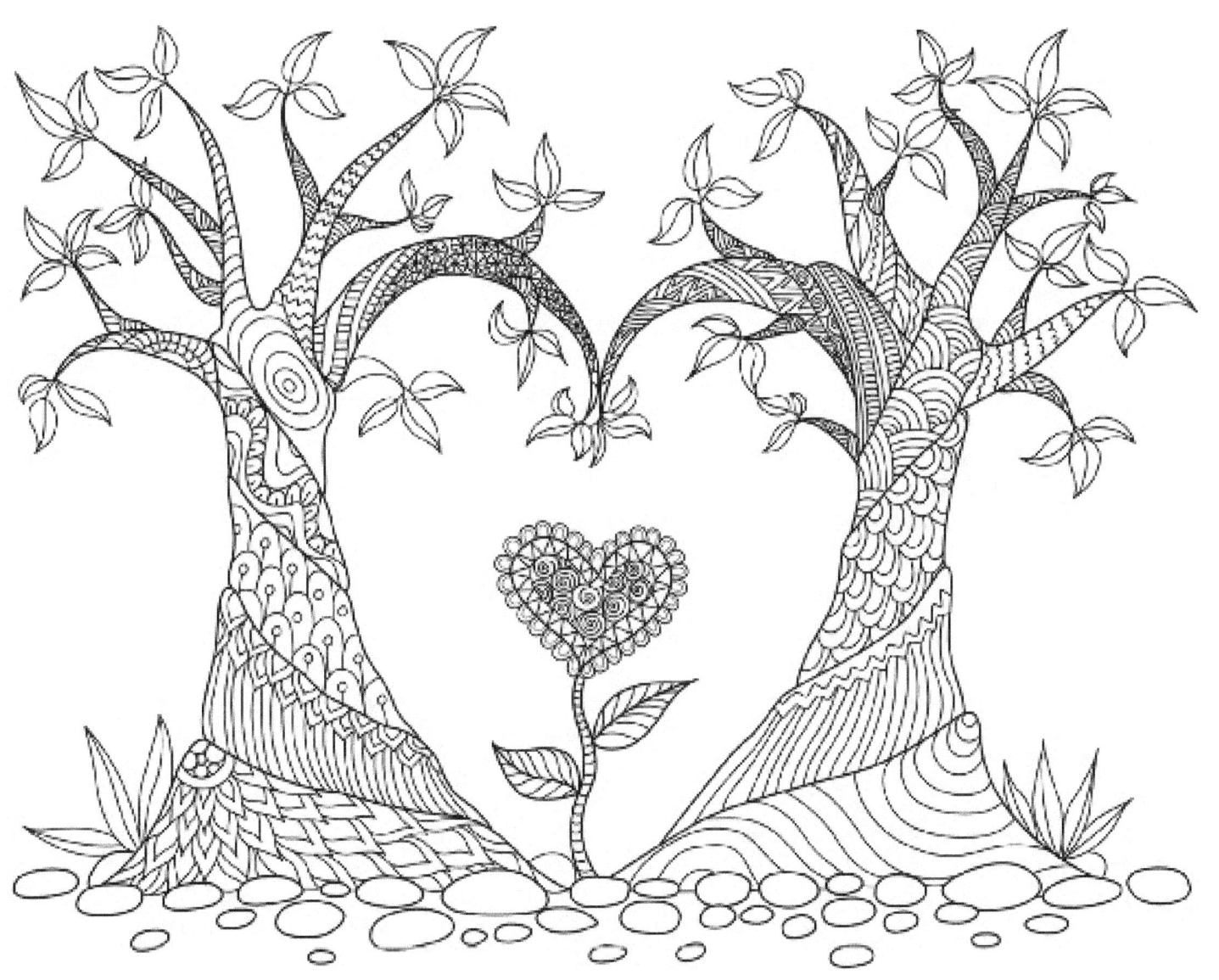

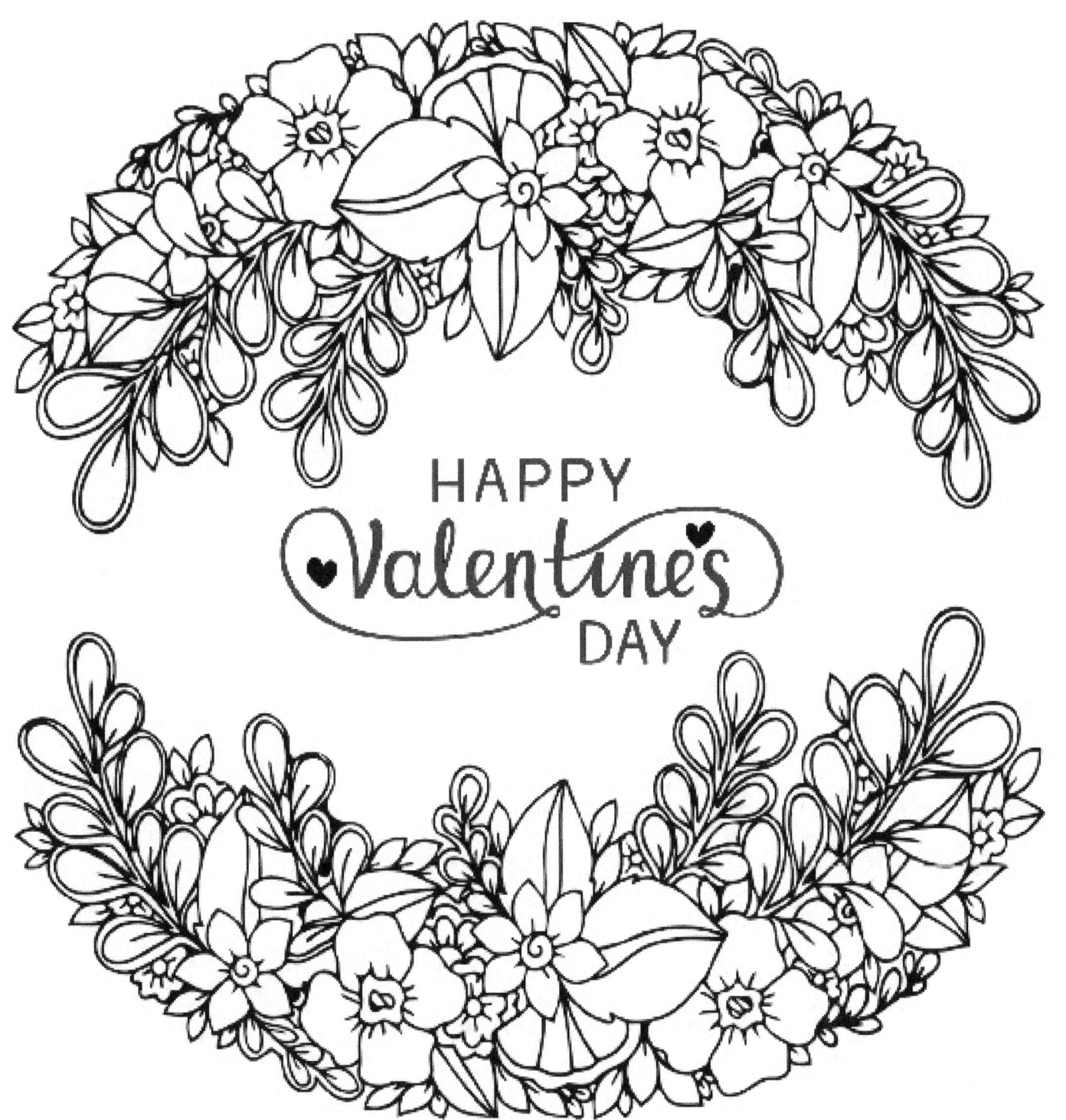

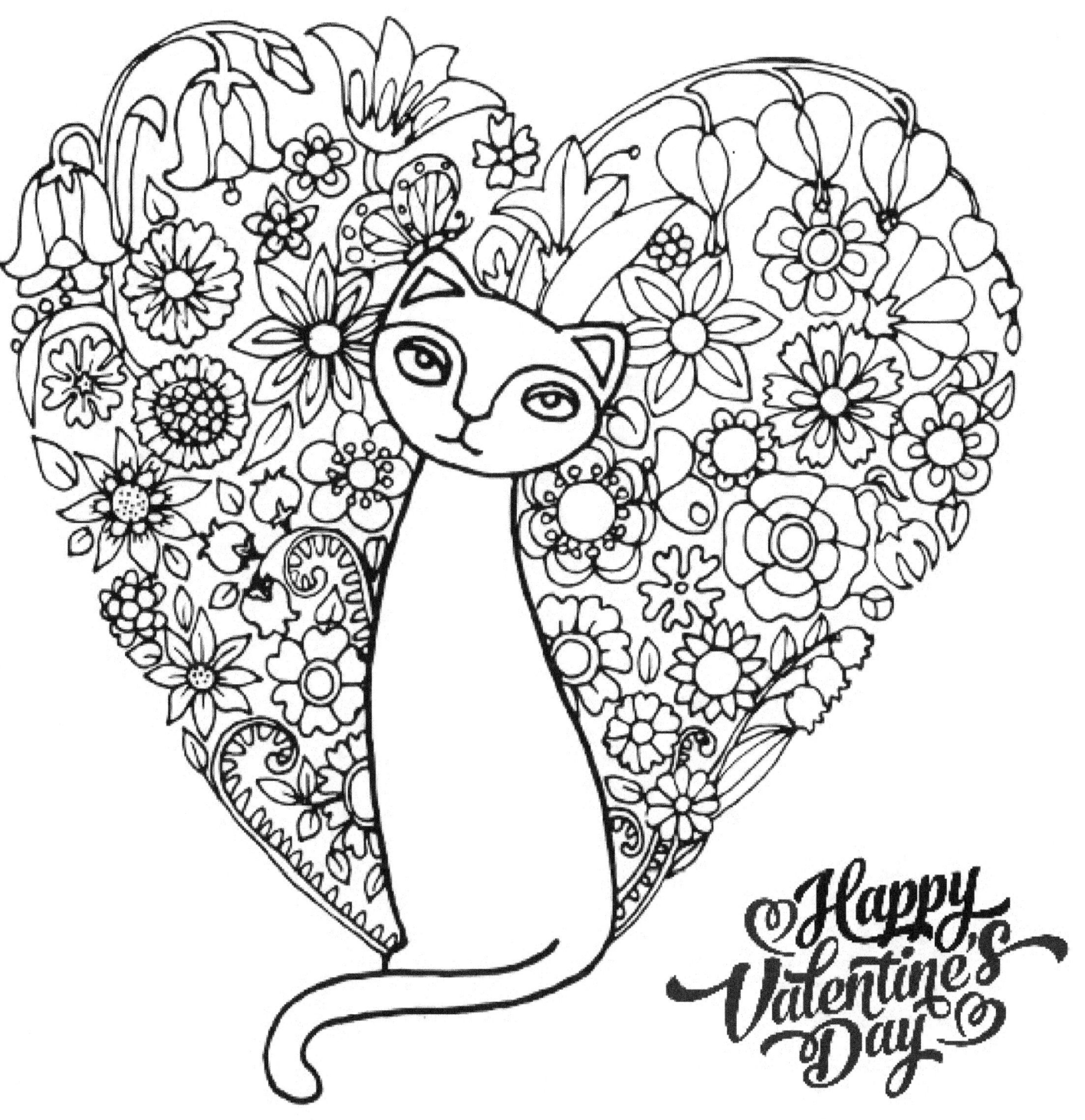

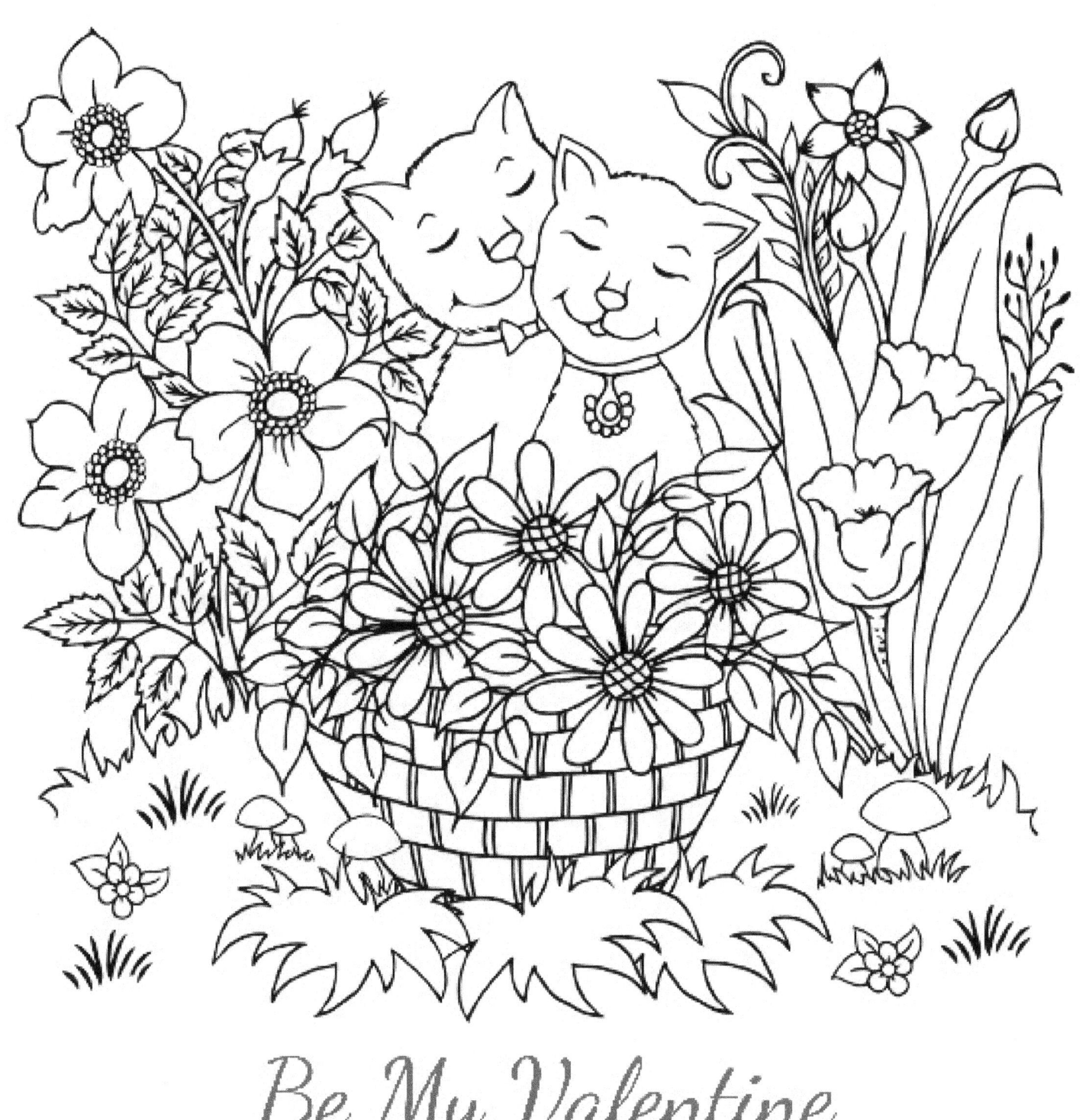

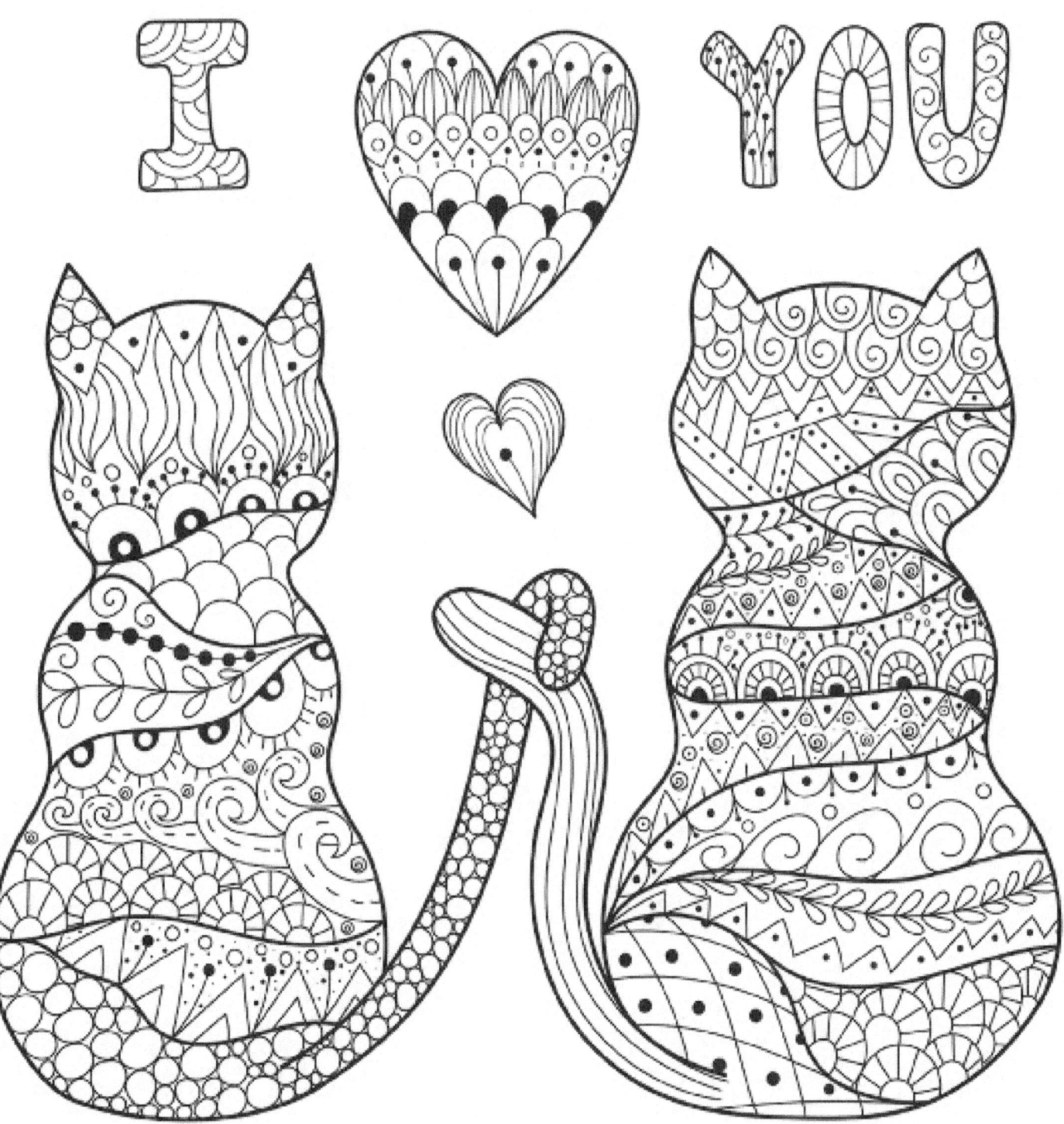

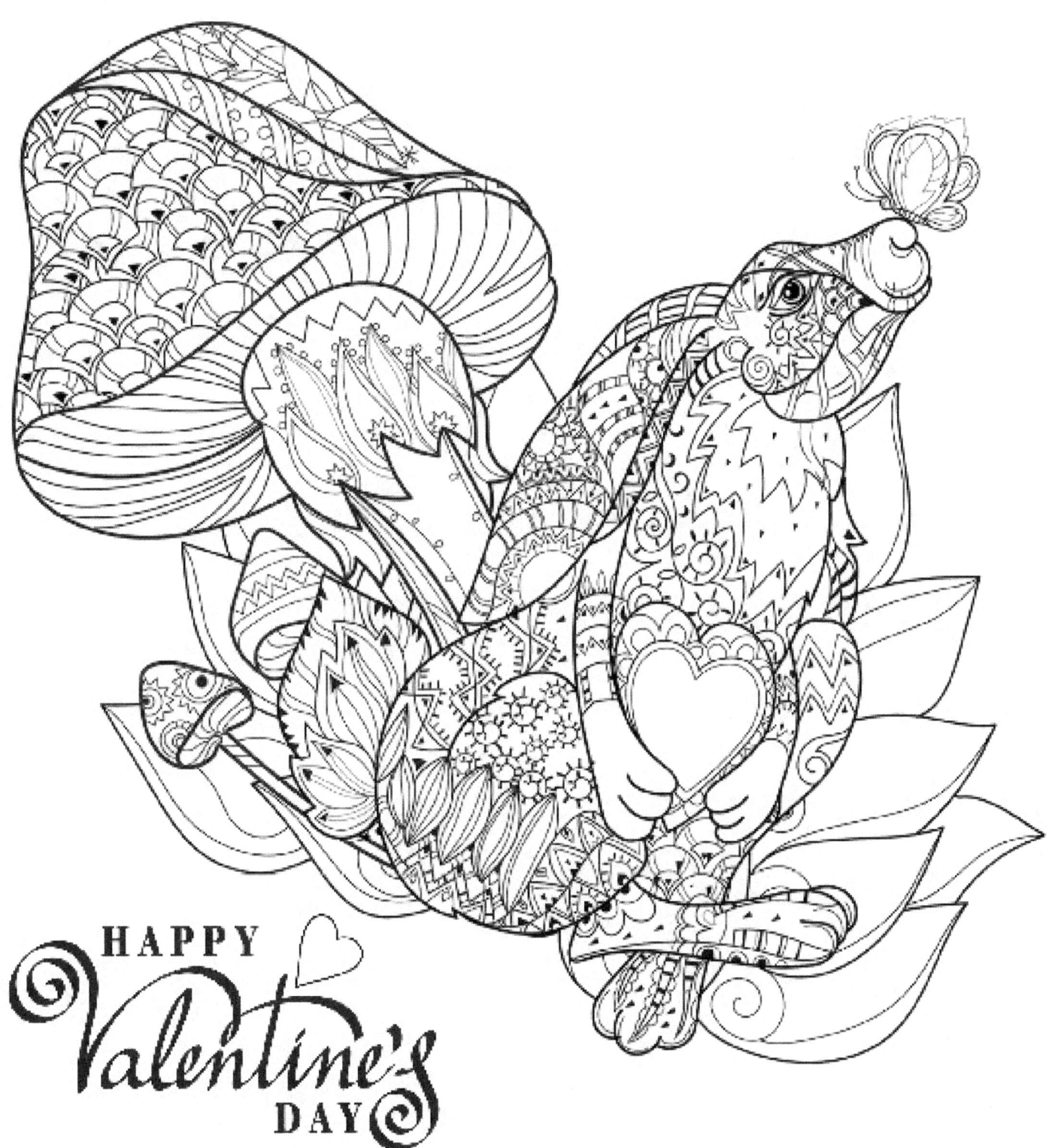

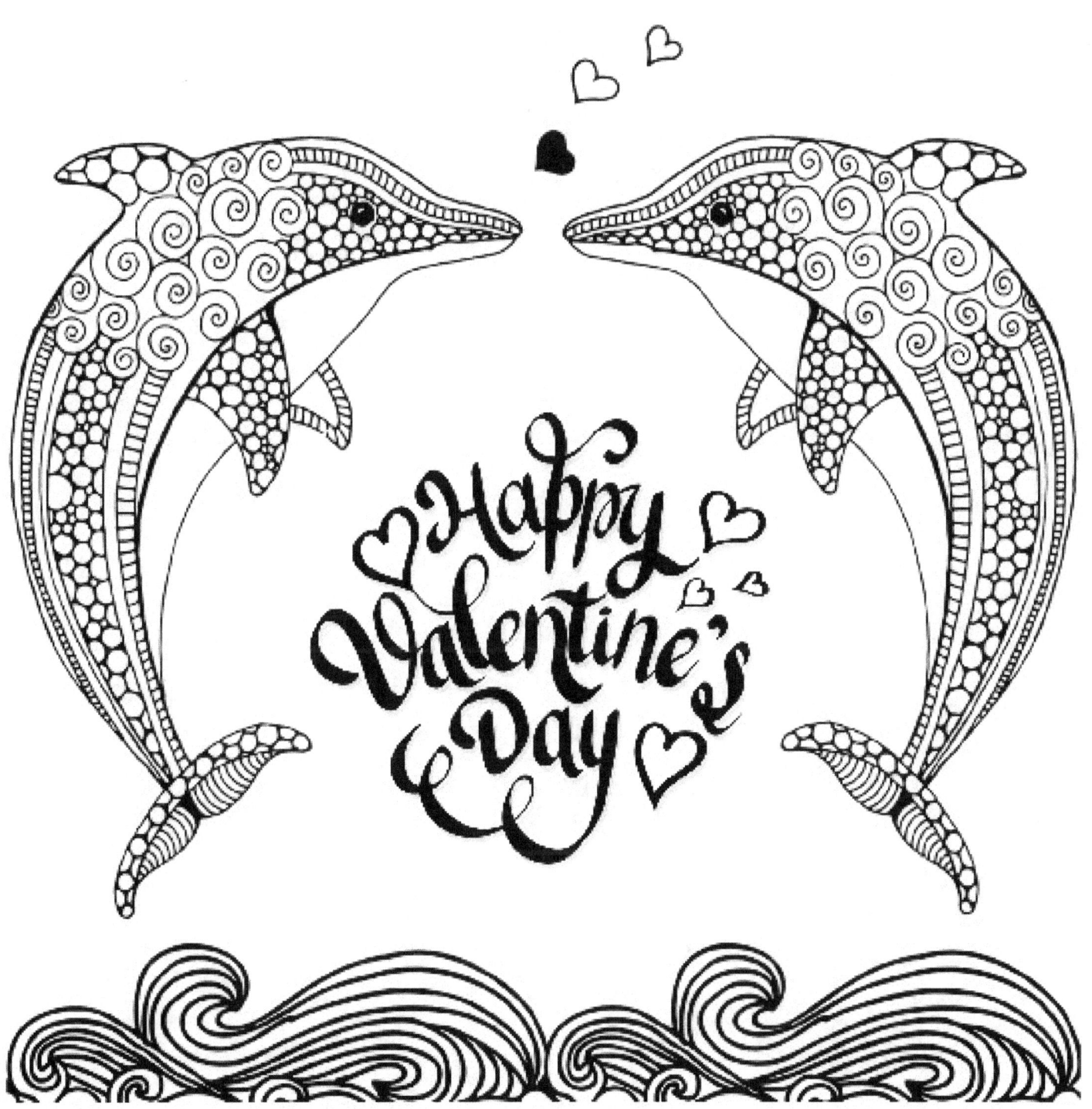

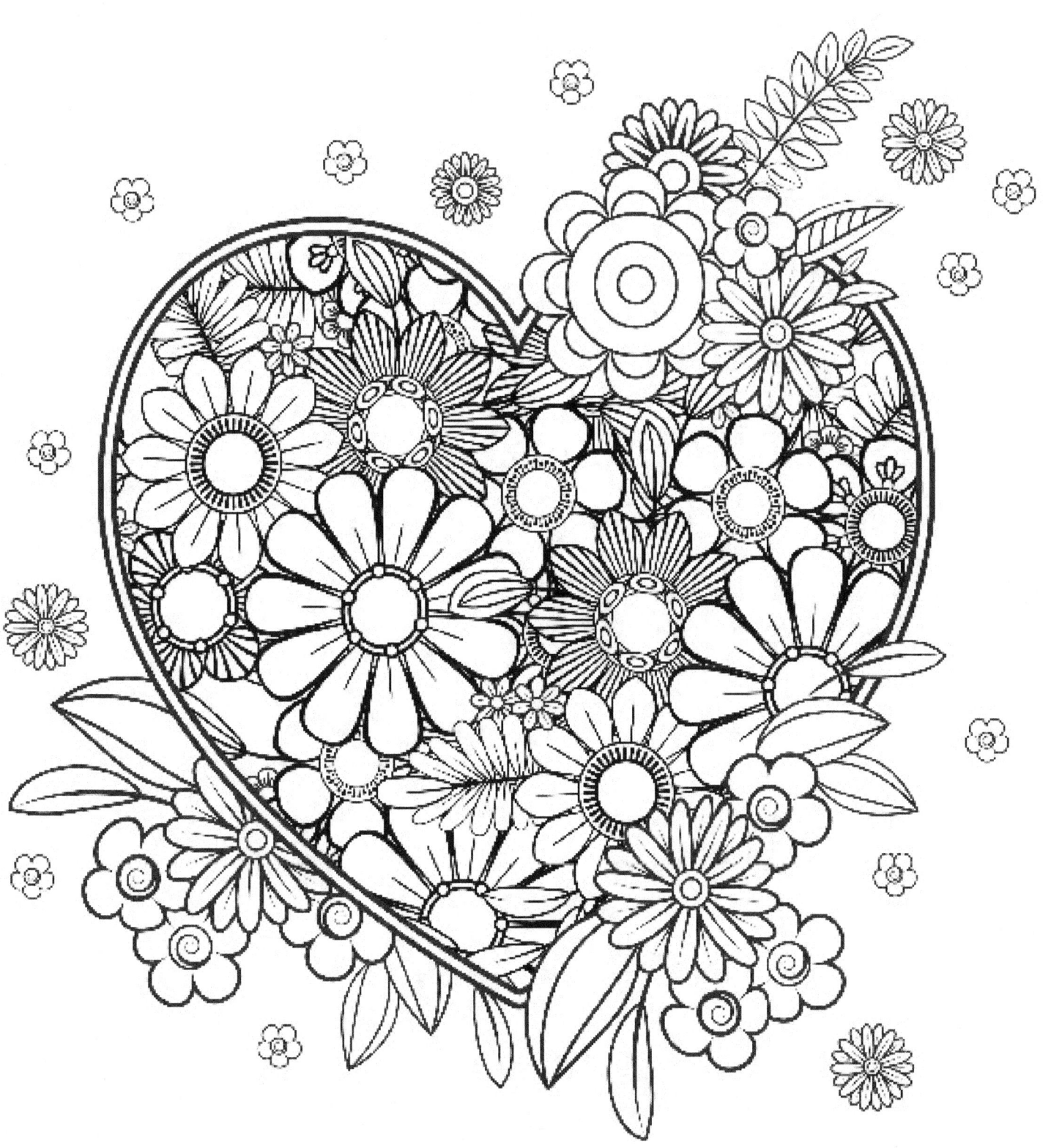

www.ingramcontent.com/pod-product-compliance
Lightning Source LLC
Chambersburg PA
CBHW060430220526

45465CB00008B/3082